E.

"Why are there no academic classes to teach us how to network effectively? This book is a training that everyone should take regardless of age! It outlines a practical, easy-to-execute set of seven steps to network like a champ, even if you are an introverted/shy person! If you want to learn how to be a networking farmer (not a hunter) and avoid the typical business pick-up lines, I highly recommend reading this book. It's a game-changer!"

—**Ken Wentworth** - Award-Winning Host of Mr. Biz Radio, 3x Best-Selling Author

"I met Chris Borja several years ago when he first started Become a Better Networker! He has inspired many to network, including myself. You might even say he's the first person who made me truly realize the power of networking! The process Chris teaches in this book will help you grow personally and professionally. Whether you're new to networking or a seasoned pro, I highly recommend it!"

—**Debra Mathias** – CEO, Connect to Clients, LinkedIn Trainer, and Career Coach

"A number of years ago, after relocating back to Columbus, Ohio from Atlanta, Georgia, I was informed that I needed to meet Chris Borja, the "Networking King" of Central Ohio! Chris is a GIVER and my kind of professional. He is an incredible asset to the community, and I'm honored to know him. I have always encouraged small business owners and professionals to get out and broaden their network in the spirit of collaboration. That's what this book is all about! Well worth the read!"

—**Sunny Martin** - Multimillion-Dollar Business Founder & Coach | Publisher of 65 Books

"I met Chris at a networking event in 2012 when he was new to networking, and I was new to town. I've seen first-hand how much he has grown in confidence, influence, and impact over the years! As a direct sales and network marketing pro, I appreciate Chris' approach to achieving results through building genuine relationships. Chris doesn't teach from theory. He teaches from experience and results! This book is a must-read for anyone in the industry looking for a fun and rejection-free way of growing their business."

—**Roland Manny** – 27-year Network Marketing Professional | Millionaire Club Member | Transformational Speaker | Trainer | Coach

"When you strip it all away and get rid of the business BS, you realize we are all just human. People with dreams in the pursuit of purpose. The business leaders, small business owners, and entrepreneurs who can see the best in people, identify common ground, link unique skill sets, and experience joy in helping others win at business and in life! Chris truly gets that networking done wrong is fake and counterproductive, but done with intentionality, skill, and genuine care, it can be the most powerful business accelerator (and impact creator) there is! He is an expert because he challenged himself and lived out his own values and beliefs. This book is written out of his desire to help others achieve their dreams."

—**Matt Davis** - CEO, COhatch

"This book is a game changer for all those who network. Whether you are a novice or a seasoned networker, there is something to be gained as a result of reading each chapter. I highly recommend Networking Essentials for Success and encourage everyone to not only get their copy, but to highlight the many golden nuggets contained within."

—**Mary Jenkins** - CEO & Founder, The (COC) Cancer Option Collaborative | 2x Breast Cancer Survivor | Cancer Patient Advocate | Motivational Speaker | Author | Evangelist | Veteran

"If you're looking to become proficient at networking, Chris Borja is the perfect person to learn from. In Networking Essentials for Success, he takes you on the same journey he took to go from being an introvert that was clueless about the value of relationships to a person who's built an expansive community of successful entrepreneurs, sales representatives, and professionals. Dig into this book and embrace yourself for a wonderful ride to great success."

—Frank Agin – Author – "Foundational Networking" | Founder and President - AmSpirit Business Connections | Host – Networking Rx Podcast | Founder - The Charitable Roundtable

"Whether you're a seasoned networker, or just getting started, this book has something in it for you! As an extrovert and natural connector, I've always enjoyed and excelled at networking. That being said, I've still learned a great deal from Chris Borja over the years, helping me to become an even better networker. Easy read and worth your time."

—Renee Vidor - Founder of The Winner's Circle Community | Author of "Measuring Up: How to WIN in a World of Comparison'"

Networking
Essentials for Success

A 7-Step Journey to Accomplishing Your
Goals Through Authentic Relationships
and Connected Communities

By Chris Borja

Published by Author Academy Elite
PO Box 43, Powell, OH 43065
www.AuthorAcademyElite.com

Identifiers:
LCCN: 2022923976
ISBN: 979-8-88583-177-2 (paperback)
ISBN: 979-8-88583-178-9 (hardback)
ISBN: 979-8-88583-179-6 (ebook)

Available in paperback, hardback, e-book, and audiobook

DEDICATION

This book is dedicated to my wife and best friend Belinda for her love, encouragement, and always being by my side, our kids Noah and Zoe for giving us so much joy, my mom for her support and unconditional love, and my dad for showing me how to live a life of service and how to raise a happy family.

TABLE OF CONTENTS

Step 1: Gain Clarity

Step 2: Adopt a Healthy Mindset

Step 3: Setup Your Systems and Tools

Step 4: Meet New People

Step 5: Develop Strong Relationships

Step 6: Build your Personal Brand and Community

***Step 7: Create Winning Collaborations
and Partnerships***

FOREWORD

I noticed a shy man sitting in my business seminar one Friday morning at the Entrepreneurial Center. After my presentation, he approached me with a warm handshake. I felt his sincerity and experienced his emotional intelligence immediately. At that moment, I decided I liked Chris Borja.

Chris kept on attending my monthly gatherings. He "showed-up filled-up" and reported on his progress in implementing the lessons every time. I never witnessed such hunger and discipline to implement. Each month, Chris' influence, impact, and income grew consistently, like the success that follows him wherever he goes.

I saw him launch products and programs. He pivoted according to the changes in the marketplace. He created collaborations and partnered with like-minded professionals. He mastered social media platforms and created technological solutions for real-world problems.

Fast-forward several years, and this unassuming, quiet influencer has emerged in our city and around the country as one of the leading practitioners on creating communities. Even the pandemic didn't stand a chance at extinguishing the fire Chris and his wife Belinda embodied.

When he talked about writing a book, I hoped he would publish it with my company. I knew Chris would deliver serious value, and I love to partner with people who truly care about others.

As one of his readers, consider yourself blessed to have his process. I know I feel this way. Many people talk about networking and connection. Most do it wrong. Chris is one of the bright lights in this space. His methods and mindset will save you serious time in achieving your goals.

He will demystify the process and show you the way. Everyone I know who knows Chris Borja is a better person and a better professional because of him. Get ready to grow yourself and your relationships. There's a much bigger world than you can imagine.

It's just one connection away.

Kary Oberbrunner
Wall Street Journal and USA Today Bestselling Author of
12 Books
CEO of Igniting Souls and Blockchain Life

INTRODUCTION

Think of a time when you were searching for a new job, looking to find new clients for your business, or moving into a new city where you didn't know anyone.

A friend or family member probably told you to "Get out there and network!"

The problem is that while you understood the concept, you probably needed to learn how to get started.

Isn't it crazy that regardless of how long we went to school, whether it be 8 years, 12 years, or even 20+ years, not a single class on "networking" is offered as part of the curriculum?

It's a critical business and life skill, but most were never taught how to do it.

As a result, networking is an activity that many business professionals rank as one of their greatest fears, right up there with public speaking!

In this book, I will take you on a 7-step journey that will eliminate your fear, increase your confidence, and help you accomplish your goals through building authentic relationships and connected communities.

Each of these steps is broken down into small bite-sized chapters that will include stories, examples, and action steps to help you network like a pro, even if you are completely new to it.

I want you to understand that I am not a natural "networker." Even to this day, I am nowhere close to what you would consider a "social butterfly."

In fact, I was a very shy introvert for the first 37 years of my life!

I would avoid social settings and speaking opportunities at all costs. Any excuse would do.

I was the kid in class who wouldn't raise his hand even though he knew the correct answer out of fear of being the center of attention or judged by his peers.

Throughout my work life, I was passed up on promotions in my retail management job because I didn't know how to represent myself and speak up.

At my best friend's wedding, I was the best man, and when it came time to give the speech, I didn't stand up. So instead, his cousin had to give the speech!

You get the point. I was not just extremely introverted but also shy on top of it. It negatively affected me throughout my life, costing me many opportunities.

But I knew I was made for more than this. I believe that God had a greater purpose for me. I had visions of speaking in front of thousands, even though I feared speaking in front of the smallest of groups.

So, I decided to stop playing small. Instead of finding excuses, I would say "yes" to the opportunities that would make me uncomfortable and help me grow.

A few years later, I discovered the world of "networking" as I sought to generate prospects for my direct sales business.

I was nervous because I had no clue what I was doing, but I found hope! I saw people thriving in their businesses, and it looked "easy" because people would come to them regularly to provide referrals!

I was looking for a better way of growing my business without calling 50 random strangers a day, getting hung up on, ghosted, and drained of all my energy, causing me to want to quit!

Purchasing "qualified" leads didn't work either, and it turned out to be a big waste of thousands of dollars in addition to the countless hours, weeks, and months chasing them down.

Additionally, I couldn't stand the feeling of always being in "prospecting" mode, whether running errands, shopping for groceries, or having dinner at a family restaurant. It was mentally and physically exhausting constantly thinking of the "pick up line" I would use to give my business card out.

I followed many gurus who would supposedly help me "build my brand on social media" and have thousands of followers begging me to buy my products. None of it worked! At least not for me.

My frustration continued to grow. I felt like I was a hard worker. I followed the programs, sincerely cared about making a difference, and believed in my product. Still no results!

Can you relate to any of this?

When I first started networking, I was doing it wrong. And it took me several months to discover that I was doing it wrong.

Finally, I took some time to slow down and evaluate the results I was generating. My sales had increased slightly due to the increased number of people I met at different networking events, but it didn't reflect the additional time and effort I was putting in.

Here's where I messed up. I wasn't really networking. Instead, I was trying to prospect and sell at networking events.

Consider this. If everyone comes to a networking event to promote or sell something, and nobody intends to buy anything, how could this situation be fruitful?

Instead of continuing this insanity, I decided to change my strategy. Instead of joining networking events to sell products, I did something much more natural. I started serving and helping people.

Being more service focused totally changed my approach. When I met new people, I would listen to get to know them. I would get to know the person BEHIND the title. This allowed me to build authentic relationships and helped my network to grow much faster.

As my network grew, I made mutually beneficial connections for those within my community.

In 2013, I stepped out of my comfort zone. I started my own networking group to make it easier for shy, introverted people like myself to meet others in a comfortable environment. This turned out to be beneficial for everyone in attendance!

In 2014, I recognized that I wasn't alone in my journey of being clueless about how to network. Many people struggled just like I did. So, I started a training company called Become a Better Networker.

At the time of writing this book, my training has served over 275,000 people across twenty-nine countries and six continents! This book is the catalyst of a worldwide movement to unite millions of people worldwide to collaborate, serve and support one another.

One of the vehicles to accomplish this worldwide movement is the Connected Networking Group based out of Columbus, Ohio, which I founded with my wife, Belinda.

We are expanding to every major city worldwide, creating a space for the business community to meet, collaborate and grow.

Many networking opportunities are available daily, but unfortunately, most people miss out on them.

By applying the strategies and skills in this book, you will accomplish your goals faster than you ever thought possible. Networking saves you tons of time because you no longer need to prospect for several hours every day!

On top of achieving your goals, you will find several additional bonuses. Some of these bonuses include life-long friends, a community that respects you, unique opportunities unavailable to the general public, and the work/life balance that most only dream of.

When I started my networking journey, I would have fallen under the "desperate salesman" category. I barely made ends meet, didn't have my own car, and felt like a big phony!

At one of my lowest points, I reluctantly sold a personalized gold bracelet my parents gave me on my 16th birthday to attend a business conference in Oklahoma City.

Today, my life is much different. I no longer need to worry about my own provisions. Instead, I get to focus on serving and impacting others to help them achieve a networking breakthrough of their own.

Networking truly changed my life. It has allowed me to make a living by making a difference! I now enjoy time with my family, travel, go on impromptu weekend getaways with my wife, and enjoy my hobbies without needing to "retire."

If you were to interview a random sample of the world's elite business professionals, they would tell you that building your network is one of the most important things you can do to ensure success.

Robert Kiyosaki, the author of Rich Dad, Poor Dad, says, "The richest people in the world look for and build networks. Everyone else looks for work."

Porter Gale, author, speaker, networker, and entrepreneur, says, "Your network is your net worth."

The infamous author, salesman, and motivational speaker Zig Ziglar says, "You can have everything in life you want if you will just help enough other people get what they want."

If you ask me what "networking" can do for you, I would say, "Absolutely anything you can dare to dream!"

Networking can produce opportunities that seemingly come out of nowhere.

Here's an example. During the Pandemic, many businesses were negatively impacted or even forced to close down! Because of my network, I was introduced to a unique virtual events platform that not only helped us continue growing our networking group through the Pandemic, but it also turned into a very lucrative virtual events production company (Borja Virtual). This new venture allowed us to serve many for-profit companies, non-profit organizations, and conference organizers across the United States!

In our first 20 months, we were able to help our clients generate over two million dollars through our virtual event services while creating a healthy revenue source for ourselves along the way.

We accomplished this with zero advertising, no cold calling, and no outbound marketing! It was all accomplished through word of mouth and warm referrals. It was networking at its finest!

When I started my networking journey, I was in a new town where the only people I knew were my wife and two kids. Today I have an extensive network of thousands of business owners, entrepreneurs, authors, speakers, coaches, artists, influencers, connectors, non-profit leaders, and world changers to share resources with.

This is what networking will do for you. It will help you grow in many ways, both personally and professionally!

Here are a few examples of what you can expect from networking:

Achieve your business goals faster than ever!

Enjoy more free time to do the things you love!

Be presented with life-changing opportunities!

Make more money!

Become appreciated and respected in your community!

Create deeper relationships and genuine friendships!

Live with purpose!

Enjoy personal development and growth!

Apply what you learn from this book right away. You will be pleasantly surprised at how much improvement you'll see in as little as a day. If you consistently apply the lessons to your everyday life, your life will be unrecognizable twelve months from now!

This book will make a tremendous impact on your business, your career, your community, and your life.

The framework is a 7-step process that walks you through every detail, starting with gaining clarity, developing a mindset for success, "working" events, developing strong relationships, building your brand, and creating winning partnerships.

It is written in a way that breaks down the process into small and easy-to-follow bite-sized steps. There are areas in this book where you will need to complete an activity. For the best results, follow each set of instructions and invest the time to complete each step because each builds on the previous step.

These chapters are filled with interesting stories and real-world examples that will open your mind to see new possibilities for yourself.

Let's dig in. I look forward to guiding you on this exciting new journey!

Step 1
Gain Clarity

Chapter 1

Why Clarity is Important

Shortly after getting married, my wife Belinda and I moved to Marina Del Rey, just south of Venice Beach and Santa Monica in the Los Angeles area of Southern California.

Being close to the beach alongside the Pacific Ocean, there was often heavy fog in the early morning and late evening hours. At times, the fog was so thick that I could barely see the traffic lights until I was right underneath them!

With limited visibility, I couldn't see very far ahead, and I definitely couldn't see my destination! So I slowed the car down and focused my attention on the dividing lines.

I used them as a guide to ensure I didn't run off the road or head into opposing traffic! I followed the lines and trusted that the road I was on would take me where I needed to go.

When you get clear on your purpose and goals, that clarity acts like those lines on the road taking you toward your destination.

This book provides the map to your journey and helps you reach your goals faster by knowing your path and the exact steps to take along the way.

Here are the 20 questions for clarity. Take the time to complete the answers because it will make all of the future steps much easier!

Some questions are designed to help you connect with potential clients and referral partners.

Some of the questions aren't directly related to your professional goals but will help you know yourself better and improve your ability to connect with others and build authentic relationships.

Your answers will play a key role in your Elevator Speech/Introduction, Branding, Social Media profiles, Goals, and Partnerships.

Answer these on a separate paper or in a new document.

1. What's your short-term goal? (Less than a year)

2. What's your long-term goal? (5 years+)

3. If time and money were not an issue, what would you do on a daily basis?

4. What are your current products or services?

5. Who purchases your products or services?

6. Why do they purchase it?

7. What are the main benefits from purchasing your products or services?

8. What are the problems you solve through your products or services?

9. What has kept you from your goals so far?

10. Who can help you reach your goals faster?

11. What is the positive impact on you, your family, and your community by reaching your goals?

12. What is the negative impact on you, your family, and your community by not achieving your goals?

13. What life event has impacted you the most in a positive way?

14. What life event has impacted you the most in a negative way?

15. What are you most proud of about yourself?

16. What are you most disappointed of about yourself?

17. How do other people describe you currently?

18. How would you like other people to describe you in the future?

19. Describe your ideal client.

20. Describe your ideal referral partner.

Chapter 2

What Are Your Goals?

In this chapter, you get to select your destination. This will be fun as you begin to dream, hope, and visualize the possibilities ahead!

It may also be frustrating at times because many people get caught up in the rat race, resulting in tunnel vision and getting stuck in survival mode.

Some people haven't slowed down to think of where they want to go because they have "failed" so often that it almost hurts to dream again. I can completely relate! I would find myself playing small for so long that it became a habit!

To help set you up for success in this chapter, I challenge you to delete any of your past failed ventures mentally. Silence the voices of "haters" or even loved ones who doubt you and discourage you from chasing your big goals and dreams.

Here's one way to remove another obstacle to achieving your goals. Answer this question. What would you set out to accomplish if time and money were not an issue and failure was not possible?

Take some time to write down the following goals. Use a separate notepad.

What are your BIG goals over the next 5 to 10 years?

What are your mid-range goals over the next 1-3 years?

What are your short-term goals over the next 1-3 months?

What are your lifestyle goals?

What are your financial goals?

What are your family goals?

What are your fitness and health goals?

What are your spiritual goals?

What other goals would you like to achieve?

Why are the above goals important to you?

These goals are your destination. Everything you do in the subsequent chapters will get you closer to your destination.

Take a few minutes to complete the answers to these questions, then proceed to the next chapter.

Chapter 3

What Has Kept You from Your Goals So Far?

What has kept you from your goals so far? It's important to address this question upfront.

Time flies and life goes by fast in today's busy world. If we don't slow down and evaluate these things, we can end up going in circles or, even worse, going in the wrong direction without realizing it!

When we don't hit our goals, it can become easy to cast blame and responsibility on something over which we have no control.

While that might be a great short-term fix to make us feel better, like "it's not my fault," the problem is that we also give up control in reaching our destiny.

Let's take an objective look at what has kept you from your goals thus far. What's in the gap?

Usually, it's something that you are missing or lacking. And the good news is that, in most cases, it's something we can control! The first step is to be aware of it.

Concerning achieving your goals, which one(s) of the following are you lacking? Which one(s) are in the gap?

Capital (Finances)?

Knowledge?

Skills?

Confidence (Fear)?

Access?

Team?

Support?

Encouragement?

Take a few minutes to write down your answers next to these categories. Feel free to add your own as needed.

Circle the ones that can be resolved by having the right people by your side.

How many of the items above could be addressed with the support of the right people?

This is where networking comes in. Networking gives you access to people who can help you on your journey!

Before the modern age of computers, smartphones, and GPS systems, we used to navigate the roads with a paper map or stopping at a gas station to ask for directions!

Meeting new people on your networking journey is like stopping to see the person at the gas station who can provide local directions because of their knowledge.

So whatever you're missing, or whatever is in the gap, people are the answer!

Chapter 4

Who Can Help You Reach Your Goals?

The interesting thing about networking is that you don't always need to meet the "highest-ranking person" to help you.

In the last chapter, we didn't need the city's mayor to give us directions. We simply needed someone who lived locally and who knew the streets. The gas station attendant was sufficient for what we needed.

Sometimes, we must reach the decision maker, the CEO, or "the boss."

Networking can provide a direct path to them (which we will cover in later chapters) or an indirect path.

But first, let's get clear on who you want to meet.

Answer the questions below.

Who is your ideal connection or client? Why?

Who can fill one of the gaps or missing links to help you achieve your goal?

Is it a specific person?

Is it someone in a particular role or position?

Is it someone with certain resources?

Write down who this person is or who these people are.

Now that you've completed this section, you know with clarity who you want to get in touch with.

Next, think of the indirect ways you can get connected with that person.

For example, you may not have direct access to the CEO of a large corporation, but you may know someone who works at that company that could make an introduction.

Before continuing to the next chapter, list the people you want to get in touch with and the people who can connect you with them. This list will be helpful in the upcoming chapters.

Chapter 5

What Do You Have to Offer?

Many new networkers have a common challenge of feeling like they don't have much to offer.

They may feel like they aren't educated or talented enough. Or maybe they don't have anything interesting to talk about. They may feel like they aren't good enough or make enough money to fit in with a particular group.

On top of that, they often feel like everyone else has everything together and already has everything they need.

The reality is that everyone has a need.

Regarding networking, the value we provide often differs from the products, services, or goods we are trying to sell.

In this chapter, we will help you to identify the value that you offer, even if you feel like you don't have anything to offer.

Let's start with the easy one. What products, services, or goods do you offer?

How are these helpful to your clients? What problems do your clients have that your products, services, and goods can solve? How would they be negatively impacted if they never found your solution?

Is what you have to offer helpful to your client? If yes, why? If not, why not?

Statistically speaking, the majority of the people that you encounter will not need your specific products, services, or goods at the moment you meet them.

If they don't need what you offer, what value are you to them?

Remember the example of the gas station attendant. They didn't need to become your client to be valuable to you. They simply needed to be familiar with the local streets to provide value to you!

In this next segment, let's explore additional ways to provide the value you may have overlooked. Invest the time to answer each of the questions below, as it will allow you to recognize things others would appreciate or relate to.

What are some of the accomplishments and awards you may have received (no matter how small you thought they were)? You may have won the spelling bee in 7th grade, received a perfect attendance award, set the school record in varsity track, or been selected as Employee of the Month or Top Sales Performer.

What are some life experiences that give you unique insights? For example, I was uncomfortable meeting new people for most of my life, so I designed special programs and training that enabled people to overcome networking fears.

What degrees, special training, or education do you have?

What relationships or connections do you have with influential leaders in your community?

What are some unique personality traits that you have that people have commented on or complimented you on? Maybe you're funny and make people laugh. Or maybe you are an extrovert and add energy to any room. Perhaps you are confident, loyal, trustworthy, resourceful, encouraging, etc.

It should give you more confidence when you itemize all the different things about yourself that provide value. Interestingly, most of the value you provide will be something other than your products, services, or goods!

I'm sure you can think of people in your life who are of value to you, even though you are not a customer or client of theirs.

This helps you see that your value goes well beyond your products and services!

Chapter 6

Knowing Yourself and Being Yourself

Many of us have heard the saying that success leaves clues. I believe that to be true!

The problem, however, is that this can lead us down the path of being something we're not.

There are times when that can be a good thing as we aspire to improve, grow and elevate our life. It can also be harmful if we try to become inauthentic to our true selves.

For as long as I can remember, I knew I wanted to have a career helping people and making a difference. In college, I studied psychology and sociology with the hopes of going into some type of counseling as a career.

But with only a bachelor's degree, I didn't have that option without an additional two years to get an entry-level job in that field. So, upon graduating, I went into retail management because that was the only opportunity that presented itself at the time.

After a few years of retail management, I expanded into direct sales and network marketing.

It was this new venture that got me started in self-development. I loved learning from so many successful people. I started reading books and attending seminars to continue my journey to grow as a person and increase sales for my business.

As I continued learning from various mentors, I encountered conflicts in their philosophies and strategies. I found myself in no man's land, attempting to follow too many different voices without getting any results.

I struggled for several years, taking training after training and course after course to boost my sales. As digital marketing grew in popularity, I tried to follow each trend, including email marketing, becoming an Instagram™ influencer, Facebook ad strategies, funnel building, and many more.

Those strategies helped but didn't work as advertised in most cases. I just ended up spending lots of time and money trying to find success in different directions.

In 2012 I attended my very first networking event. It was intimidating since I had no idea what I was doing. At this networking event, I saw a few people doing business differently than I did.

As a result of the trust they had built with others, I saw them being approached throughout the event and offered referrals on the spot!

I was thinking, "If people came to me with referrals, I'm sure I would have a lot more sales!" It seemed much easier than all of the "prospecting" I had unsuccessfully done for years!

So my new journey began. I started networking anywhere and everywhere. When I first started networking, my goal was to meet new people, get their contact information, and send them an invitation to attend a sales presentation or a one-on-one.

I was taught that the more presentations you make, the more sales you ultimately get. While there's truth to it, that philosophy has a drawback.

The drawback is a big one. This style of prospecting tends to treat people as numbers. I remember being taught the saying, "Some will, some won't, so what. Next."

I understand that from a sales standpoint, you are trying to sift and sort through the numbers to find qualified prospects, meet with them, show your product and move on.

I followed this philosophy and attempted to call, message, or email 50 people daily!

My sales increased slightly from the number of people I reached out to. However, it left me exhausted and drained at the end of the day.

I also hated the fact that I felt like I never had time off. Typically, dinner time for most families, between 5 and 7 pm, was also prime time for calling because that was when people were getting home from work.

Whenever we went out, I was always in "prospecting" mode. Whether it was the friendly server at the restaurant, the cashier, the person I stood next to in line, or anyone I was around. My brain was always thinking about my "business pick-up line." How would I give them my business card and tell them about what I do?

I did this for several years without any breakthroughs. I took this strategy into the networking world because that was all I had known. That's what the successful people in my company were doing. The problem was it just wasn't me.

So back to the networking events. As I met people at the events, I did not listen to what they had to say. I was too focused on what I would say and how I would "wow" them quickly so they would be interested in purchasing my products!

I was just looking for more prospects for my business. In my sales training, I was taught to build rapport. I was taught things like complimenting them on their shoes, outfit, or hair. After all, people love being complimented!

But, there was something that felt disingenuous because my main goal was to get their contact info so I could send a pitch or set a follow-up appointment to give my sales presentation.

As I continued with this strategy, I found that I would often have people ignore my calls, voicemails, and emails without even sending a simple response that they were not interested.

Since my sales training had taught me that fortune is in the follow-up and that we should follow up until they buy or die, I had more and more people I was following up with and more and more people who were not returning my messages.

As I went to events and would inevitably see someone I had been following up with, we both experienced awkwardness because they had ignored my messages! Now we had run into each other at the event. It was more like we pretended not to see each other to avoid an awkward conversation.

I knew something didn't feel right, but this was all I learned how to do. It was all I had been taught. I wanted to follow other successful people, and this was what they said they did, but it wasn't working for me at all.

After about a year of networking in this fashion, I learned from other professionals who had built their businesses through networking. I had to stop and ask myself, "If people aren't coming to networking events to buy from me, and everyone is there to sell their services or goods, how can this be effective?"

So I changed my method of operation.

For years, I had been networking with a method that simply wasn't "me". I was only doing it because I was told this was how you become successful. Even though some people have achieved great success with this type of prospecting, I found that it wasn't for everyone, especially not for people like me.

I could see that I would never reach the top continuing to do what I had been doing unsuccessfully for years. I was not the real me, and it came across subconsciously to my prospects.

The decision was made to help people in any way I could, whether it involved a product or not. This shifted my mindset to focusing on other people's needs before my own. When I made this shift, I was operating authentically as the person I truly was: someone who wanted to help.

Because I was no longer focused on myself and how I would turn a conversation into a possible sale for me, I could focus on the other person! I listened intently to get to know them better and learn more about what they were looking to accomplish, who they were looking to meet, and who would make a good prospect for their business.

The conversations were so focused on the other person that there were times when I didn't even introduce my own business because they didn't ask.

As I helped them with connections and resources to reach their goals, I started creating genuine relationships and friendships.

This all came much more naturally to me. I was just helping others without any hidden motives or personal objectives.

Because of the relationships that I built, I started receiving referrals regularly. It changed my business results tremendously!

Now, when I walked into a room, instead of being ignored, I would receive a happy greeting along with a handshake or a hug!

People were happy to see me, and I was delighted to see them! This was such a refreshing change compared to my old ways of prospecting.

I was still introverted, which some might think would be detrimental to someone becoming a good networker.

It would be tough to become an extrovert if I'm truly an introvert and vice versa. So instead, I embraced my introverted traits and used them to my advantage.

While extroverts would be naturally comfortable in a large group setting, I was more comfortable in a small or intimate setting. Knowing this, I would meet people in smaller groups and then meet for a one-to-one conversation which was much more up my alley.

As an introvert, I didn't feel the need to be the one talking most of the time. I felt completely comfortable asking questions and listening to the answers. As a result, I learned a lot about the person I was meeting with.

Extroverts are great at keeping the conversation going because they gain energy from the engagement and interaction. So, whether you are an introvert or an extrovert, instead of trying to be someone you are not, be yourself!

But knowing yourself and being yourself goes way beyond your prospecting philosophy or being an introvert or extrovert. This means everything about you, including your dress and talk, interests, passions, hobbies, and ambitions!

As a byproduct, being yourself provides others with the space to be who they are!

This creates a perfect environment for trust and friendship to take place. When you're authentic, you will position yourself for true connection.

Step 2
Adopt a Healthy Mindset

Chapter 7

What Networking Is and What It Isn't

For many people, networking can evoke emotions ranging from anxiety and fear to anticipation and excitement. Sometimes networking gets a bad rap because many people don't understand what it really is.

Networking events often had people in attendance like me when I first started. People like the former me are looking for a quick fix to hit a sales quota, a month-end goal, qualify for a bonus, or generate instant revenue to pay their bills. Some people are mainly concerned with finding a new job, soliciting donations, or looking to promote an upcoming event they are hosting.

While these are all excellent reasons to network, they are also short-sighted. Networking is not about passing out business cards, seeking your objectives, and giving your sales pitch to everyone in the room.

Networking is about creating genuine relationships to share resources, collaborate and create win-win situations for everyone involved. Networking is more of a team sport than it is an individual sport. It's about building community on the way to achieving your own individual goals!

> NETWORKING IS ABOUT CREATING GENUINE RELATIONSHIPS TO SHARE RESOURCES, COLLABORATE AND CREATE WIN-WIN SITUATIONS FOR EVERYONE INVOLVED.

An incorrect view of networking will affect your mindset, impacting your activity and results. Anyone who says that networking doesn't work probably has never had the correct concept of networking.

Over the following chapters, you will develop a new mindset about proper networking. This is the foundation of everything you can build for yourself and your community. You will learn from different analogies and stories that will bring this subject alive and change how you look at networking forever!

Chapter 8

How Networking Is Like Cheating in Poker

Many people conduct their business networking like playing poker, a win-lose proposition.

Proper networking is a lot more like "cheating" in poker!

Let me explain.

Imagine, for a second, a table of five poker players. They all confidently lean over their chips, doing their best to look as unemotional as possible. They glance across the table at each of the other players, reading them to get a feel for how strong their cards are.

The main objective in poker is to have the best hand.

The secondary objective is to maximize the winnings from that hand. This often involves elements of "bluffing."

Someone with a good hand may pretend not to have a good hand, and those with a poor hand will often act or try to give off signs that they do!

This is the case because, in the game of poker, there is only one winner in the end. One person wins the whole pot, and everyone else loses! It's a win-lose proposition.

Here is how networking is different from that scenario. When done correctly, it should be a win-win proposition all the time!

Imagine another poker table with five different players.

The rules they forgot at this new table were that you're not allowed to look at one another's cards, nor are you allowed to exchange cards! So they look at their five cards and realize they're missing a few select cards to complete a higher hand. Because they don't know they can't exchange cards, they all put their cards face up.

Rather than wearing dark sunglasses and trying to fool each other into thinking they have a better hand, they look at each other's cards and each other and exchange cards to improve their hands. Can you already see a big difference?

You see, what is happening is that they are now collaborating versus competing with one another!

Good networking is about collaborating. It's about sharing and exchanging resources. It's about helping other players to get a better hand. It's not about who has the highest hand. It's about the fact that everyone is a resource to someone else.

Everyone can and will improve their hand when they play as a team! Additional benefits are that they are working to serve one another. They will have a better relationship than those competing.

In this situation, everyone comes out as a winner because they all had a better hand after trading with one another than before they started.

Let's transition this analogy over into the business world. Instead of everyone looking out for their own business, needs, and priorities, what would happen if they focused on those in their community?

In the game of poker, the worst hand is to have one of each different type of card, each in a different suit. While worthless to that player, each card may be the final piece of the puzzle for other players to improve their hand to three of a kind, a flush, or even a royal flush! Working together, everyone can and will benefit.

> WORKING TOGETHER, EVERYONE CAN AND WILL BENEFIT.

When out networking, we regularly have those "cards" that may seem less important to us because they may not be our clients or customers. But they may be good clients or customers who can make a huge difference for someone else in our network! Who knows, it might be their next multimillion-dollar contract!

Let's say, for example, that you did help somebody else to complete their royal flush. Can you imagine how thankful they would be for you sharing that resource with them? What do you think they might do for you to show their appreciation? Do you think they could ever forget about you?

They will likely look for every opportunity to reciprocate that favor, actively looking for ways to share their resources with you to help you have a better hand!

So next time you go out and network, remember how networking is like cheating at cards!

Chapter 9

Are You a Hunter or a Farmer

When people start their networking journey, they commonly approach it like a hunter with a shotgun. They want immediate results for their effort.

Ivan Misner, Founder of the world's largest referral group known as BNI™, says, "Networking is more about farming than hunting." I agree that networking is more like farming, which requires planting seeds, care, and cultivation but results in a much greater return.

I learned this lesson the hard way. I remember going to my first networking event, looking for more leads for my business. I saw many people and opportunities to get their information and add them to my prospect list, hoping for that next sale.

I left disappointed that no one had signed up with me to be a customer.

But I realized they were there for a reason, and it wasn't to be my customer! They were there because they had their own business and they had their own interests in mind.

So, I watched and carefully observed those achieving success through networking.

Then I ran across the analogy of sowing and reaping, and it woke me up. It helped me to see things from a new perspective. For example, we know that when the farmer goes out and sows seeds, not all of them grow.

Some will fall on the surface and get eaten by the birds. Some will sprout quickly and get scorched by the sun because the roots are shallow. Some will start to grow but get choked out by the weeds. And some will land in fertile ground, flourish, and multiply 30, 60, or 100 times.

When we are out networking, we want results now. And I get it. After all, we do live in a microwave society. We want everything fast, we want our meals fast, and we want our results fast! However, the most flavorful meals are not made in the microwave.

The best meals take a long time to prepare. Sometimes it'll take days to start marinating and preparing the ingredients, but the results are incomparable.

In the same way, networking takes time to develop. Networking is about building relationships. It takes more cultivating, just like the farmer would need to protect and nourish their new seedlings for them to flourish.

The hunter may get immediate results from time to time, but there are also periods of drought where they may not catch or kill anything. They also are only as good as their "kill."

On the other hand, the farmer will produce a harvest that grows so bountiful that they will have plenty to share with neighbors and their community!

So why don't more people go out and network like the farmer? The answer is that they don't see the bigger picture. They want immediate results, and when they don't receive those results, they conclude that networking doesn't work.

That is just like the farmer putting exactly five seeds in the ground and coming back the next day, seeing that the seeds have not grown yet and thought that farming doesn't work or the seeds are no good. It's not that farming doesn't work. It simply wasn't enough time and not enough seeds!

It would also be foolish for the farmer to sit and wait for those five seeds to germinate and start to grow. You can see how frustrating that would be. Unfortunately, that's how most people approach their networking! They give up before there's any chance to experience any growth!

Discouraged, they abandon their new seeds without the nourishment and protection required to grow. Instead, they go back to hunting and rely on that as a way of life since it's all they may know.

My purpose in sharing these lessons is for you to understand the concept of networking. Hopefully, you can visualize acres and acres of healthy farmland producing crops and fruit for many generations!

Your farm may produce an abundance of a particular crop while your next-door neighbor grows a different crop. You can see how trade can quickly develop as you have an abundance of your harvest while they have an abundance of theirs!

That's what it's like to network correctly. Except, instead of crops, you'll have excellent contacts and relationships to share.

Chapter 10

Lessons from the River

Pierre is out on the shoreline fishing. Instead of a rod and reel that most of us use to fish, Pierre uses an ancient spearfishing method. Spearfishing takes an incredibly high level of skill to be successful.

First, you must be fortunate enough to be in striking range of the fish. You also need the accuracy and speed to hit the exact one you want. And once you miss, there's a good chance that the rest of the fish will scatter!

Pierre will catch two to three fish to bring home to his family on a good day. But there are also days when he doesn't catch any fish.

After many years of spearfishing, Pierre realized this ancient method wasn't doing the job. He needed to be more consistent. He could only catch so many fish with a spear.

So Pierre creates a net where he can throw it out into the water and capture a bunch of fish at once. Pierre tries it, and it works! He pulls his net in at the end of the day and finds he has 100 fish in his net! He picks the five he wants to bring back to his family and, not wanting to be wasteful, throws the other 95 fish back.

Thomas also depended on fishing to provide for his family. He went through the same journey as Pierre a hundred yards up the river, realizing spearfishing wasn't meeting his needs.

Thomas does the same thing as Pierre, building a net. He throws it into the water, also catching 100 fish. He takes five fish out of the 100 for his family and throws the rest back.

Both men continue doing this for months.

One day, they ran across each other on the trail returning to their village. After a pleasant greeting, Pierre noticed that Thomas had five good-sized trout in his basket. Looking into Thomas' basket, Pierre said, "If you want trout, I just threw a bunch of them back! My family only eats bluegill!"

Thomas noticed that Pierre had five bluegills and said, "You know what? I also caught some bluegill and threw them back into the water because my family only eats trout!"

The two men agreed to give each other the excess bluegill and trout they caught, increasing the amount of fish each man took home with the same labor.

When most people get started in networking, they use a spearfishing method. They're mainly focused on what they want and need without considering the more significant win available through collaboration, as Thomas and Pierre discovered.

Let's translate this story into a networking scenario where we meet 100 new people. Regardless of our industry, it's doubtful that all 100 would become our customers.

What do we do with everyone else that is not our customer?

In the same way that Pierre was throwing 95 of the 100 fish back into the water, we do the same with those who don't become immediate customers.

When we realize that those 95 are valuable to others around us, we can begin successful collaborations just like Pierre and Thomas.

Imagine what would happen if a dozen collaborations like this happened in your business!

Next time you go out networking, remember that each person who is not your customer still carries value and may be casting out their own net and acquiring additional resources.

Find ways to be of service and build relationships. Gather your resources. Serve and share your resources with others. Many will choose to reciprocate, resulting in more business for everyone involved in the group.

Chapter 11

Finding Your Black Belt

This lesson will help you see beyond the immediate goal of finding your ideal prospect and learn the value of everyone in your network. It will change how you view and treat people, regardless of their occupation, socioeconomic status, or appearance.

Before we jump into the black belt lesson, here's a quick story. Joe, the Realtor, attends his local networking event looking for his next client. He gets up early, brushes his teeth, shaves, takes a shower, irons his shirt, and heads out at 6:30 am to be at his 7 am networking event.

He shows up to find many well-dressed people. There's a buzz in the room as he starts to circulate. He nervously taps the stack of business cards in his pocket, eager to start dealing his cards like a Las Vegas black-jack dealer.

Joe scans the room, assessing who looks like a good prospect. He engages in his first conversation. As the other person is speaking, Joe can't wait to ask the question that really matters to him, "Hey, would you happen to be looking to buy or sell a house? I'm a realtor, and if you're looking to buy or sell a home, I can help!"

How would you feel if somebody approached you in this fashion? Even if you were looking to buy or sell a home, would you be more or less likely to do business with Joe?

Well, that's an exaggerated example but not too far exaggerated. Many people approach networking in this fashion, whether they're a realtor, mortgage loan officer, financial planner, entrepreneur, small business owner, multi-level marketing rep, or non-profit leader.

I've helped people avoid this tendency to be self-focused and self-promotional through a workshop activity I call the "Networking Scavenger Hunt."

I hand out a sheet with ten categories that the participants are asked to complete by meeting other people in the room. Some of the categories are: Who drove the furthest to get to this event? Who has the most pets? Who has been to most states in the United States? Who has a black belt in martial arts? Who has jumped out of an airplane?

I give them a limited amount of time, creating an element of pressure. I hand the sheets out and tell them their time has started now! The participants typically begin speaking with the person immediately to their left or to their right.

They proceed to go down the list, asking each other all ten of the questions. After that, they duplicate the process with the person sitting on their other side.

Eventually, they realize that their neighbors don't get out as much as they should, and many of the categories remain unanswered! They then get out of their chair and explore the room, seeking people who fit the various categories.

As time begins to run out, something happens. They realize that they won't be able to get to everyone in the room in the allotted time! Now they begin circling up and asking each other who had the most traffic tickets. Or who had the most pets? In essence, they start asking for referrals!

Those who have the answers excitedly shout out the response of the person that fits that category. "John jumped out of a plane!" "Joanna has the most pets! She has seven cats!" "Susie traveled the furthest to get here! She drove 80 miles!"

They continue doing this until time runs out. I call them back to their seats, review the answers, and recap the lessons.

We went through the answers and experienced many laughs along the way. The participants had a great time connecting and having fun getting to know one another.

After going through all of the categories, there would typically be one or two categories not represented in the room. Often, there would be no one in the workshop who had a black belt in martial arts.

Here is where I begin breaking down the lessons from the activity. I share the example with them of how often we approach these networking events looking for a particular person, like Joe, the realtor.

In this situation, no one in the room had a black belt. The "black belt" represents the ideal person you are looking for at a networking event.

Based on your profession, who is it that you are looking for? Is it someone looking for a new financial plan? Is it someone looking to buy a new car? Is it someone that owns a small company and needs a new phone system or computer equipment? Or maybe it's somebody that needs a new website?

That person you are looking for, is your "black belt." Just like in the scavenger hunt activity, it's likely that your black belt is also not in the room!

There is usually a moment of silence as people absorb this lesson. They start to wonder if networking works and if it's just a waste of time.

But then, I asked them another question as they all looked up at me with eager open eyes. I asked them, "How many of you, by a show of hands, personally know someone who is a black belt in martial arts?"

Eventually, about a third of the room will raise their hands. I ask them to all look around and see how many have access to a black belt.

When we are out networking, it's not just about the person we want to meet directly. Everyone is important!

More often than not, we focus on the person we meet, hoping they become our clients.

WHEN WE ARE OUT NETWORKING, IT'S NOT JUST ABOUT THE PERSON WE WANT TO MEET DIRECTLY. EVERYONE IS IMPORTANT!

But as you can see, there were no black belts in the room. However, about a third of the people in the room had access to someone who was a black belt!

This whole time we've been struggling to search for our black belts. All we needed to do was ask one additional question, "Who do you know that's a black belt?"

We had so many participants with access to a black belt! We can now not only find a black belt in one discipline of martial arts, but if needed, we can find a black belt in several different martial arts!

Do you see how only looking for a specific prospect at an event is thinking small? Does this cause you to look at people differently because we are no longer just looking at them as numbers?

Remember how the participants started to ask for referrals in the scavenger hunt game? Who drove the furthest, who had the most pets, etc.? That's how simple it is to ask for a referral when you have the right mindset. It's as simple as asking if your new connection knows someone who fits a specific category!

It was easy to ask for referrals during the scavenger hunt game because they had no ulterior motives. They were just having fun learning about each other and helping one another!

What would it look like if you applied this to the real world?

What if, for every twelve people you talked to at a networking event or any other gathering, four can connect you with that decision-maker, business owner, client, investor, influencer, or whomever you want to meet?

Remember that we are not prospecting the other networkers. We are building relationships to see how we can best serve them so they can do likewise as they get to know, like, and trust us.

Chapter 12

Lessons from a Candle

In this chapter, you will learn the value of sharing resources and how they can impact your networking efforts.

Let's build on the last chapter with a quick mindset lesson that will transform the way you network. Remember the chapter about playing poker and sharing resources? Let's take that to the next level.

I remember attending a Christmas Eve candlelight service at church with my family. When the end of the service approached, the ushers walked up to the front, where a lit candle was gently flickering.

Each usher came to the front of the church and lit candles from this single flame, then proceeded into the aisles. As they walked through the aisles, they began by lighting the person's candle at the end of each row.

The person on the end then lit their neighbor's candle next to them. Their neighbor did the same. Each person continued until the darkened room became a beautifully glowing candle-lit church.

Looking toward the front, we could see that the original candle was still lit. That candle had lost nothing as the ushers lit their candles. As everyone passed the flame to one another, their candles remained lit.

One of my favorite sayings is, "A candle loses nothing by lighting another candle," by James Keller.

Here's how it relates to our networking mindset and subsequent results, returning to the poker analogy. Most people hold onto their cards for fear of losing something.

By not openly sharing because they fear giving up a card or two, they're actually missing out on something much better! They could be receiving cards that can improve their hand!

The same is true for the candle. Sometimes people will feel like they don't want to give something away because they fear losing that thing they're giving away.

But networking is a lot closer to this analogy of the candle. We lose nothing by sharing our resources! Our candle doesn't go out just because we help somebody light theirs. The more people we spread that light to, the bigger our impact!

To illustrate this, imagine what happens when you put the flame of two candles together. The flame doubles in size! Add a third and fourth candle together, and the size of the flame gets even taller!

A single candle at the church could light hundreds of other candles in just a few minutes. This should serve as a powerful visual of how quickly our network can spread when done correctly!

The more people within our network who are lighting other candles along with us, the faster and stronger we all grow!

Step 3
Setup Your Systems and Tools

Chapter 13

The Connected System of Success

Every four years, we experience the world's best competition in various sports at the Olympic Games. I'm inspired more by the stories of the athletes on their road to competing at the games than their performance once they are competing.

We watch the stories of their small hometown, their background starting from childhood, the hardships they encountered along the way, their perseverance in overcoming adversity, qualifying to represent their country, and finally, the opportunity to compete as one of the world's elites in their sport.

The thing that separates the medalists from the rest of the crowd is preparation.

While we see the final results of that preparation in the form of a perfect or close-to-perfect performance with all of the world watching, we don't see the hours of practice per day, the disciplined fitness regime they go through, and the strict diet required to compete at that level.

In the same way, we often see people who are successful at business but don't see all of the behind-the-scenes work, disciplines, processes, and systems they have in place to reach that level.

In this chapter, you will learn a straightforward approach that will allow you to grow your network and your business through authentic relationships and collaborative communities.

The following chapters will break each step down further so you can see the why and how for each component.

When I first started networking, I was winging it. I had no system because I didn't have a clue as to what I was doing. I just knew I needed to meet more people!

As I progressed in my networking journey, I started to perform certain habits, which was good, but I hadn't documented it.

When I began teaching others how to improve their networking skills, I created a system for people to follow to get similar results. Some components have changed because of new technologies available.

The Connected System of Success you are about to learn will position you for success by utilizing both a "high-tech" and "high-touch" approach to building relationships.

You will use technology to save time and stay organized while staying in touch with your new and old connections. You will also have a regular presence online and in person with your growing network.

At one time, Rolodex was the primary contact management system. If you talk to someone older who did business in the 90s or earlier, they probably continue to use terminology like, "Let me flip through my Rolodex." "I'll have to look through my Rolodex."

We now have several tools, such as social media, CRMs (client relationship management), email lists, and social media.

The Connected System of Success is a way to stay connected with your network, consistently build quality relationships, give first, serve your community, stay top of mind, get referrals and create opportunities for bigger wins through collaboration.

Here is an outline of the Connected System of Success components:

1. Develop your Concise Introduction, aka Elevator Speech
2. Prepare your business cards and collateral, and website
3. Set up your social media platforms (LinkedIn, Facebook, etc.)
4. Set up your calendar and contact management system
5. Attend two networking events per month, online or in person
6. Build relationships on social media. Post once per day. Do five intentional engagements with new connections and ten with your existing network
7. One-to-one calls, coffee, and lunches (at least one per week)
8. Serve and add value (one event or volunteer activity per month)
9. Host an event/gathering (1 per month)

10. Stay consistent with your brand
11. Create collaborations and partnerships

The following chapters will break down these steps to make them easy to implement and become a habit.

Chapter 14

Your Introduction, AKA "Elevator Speech"

"What do I say?"

This is one of the most common questions that new networkers have when thinking about going to a networking event or going someplace to meet new people.

Understandably, it causes tons of anxiety because we have learned that we only have one chance to make a good first impression! Many worry about fumbling for the right words, sounding too salesy, saying something stupid, or completely blanking out!

So, some resort to writing a perfectly crafted "elevator speech" to solve the problem. As a first step, it isn't bad, but what ends up happening is that it sounds completely canned, inauthentic, and not tailored to the person or audience to whom they are speaking.

We've all heard someone do this type of introduction. The person may have been confident, delivered it smoothly, and maybe even sounded good saying it, but there is something about it that just didn't connect.

The term "elevator speech" or "elevator pitch" comes from the idea that this speech or pitch is short enough to be delivered in the time that one might be in an elevator.

While this is a common term, and you will hear it often, we will provide a different name and model for it in this chapter.

Some people don't like the word "pitch" because it can come across as being salesy. Even though I am not a big fan of the terms "elevator speech" or "elevator pitch," I also don't have a problem with it. However, we will call it our introduction to improve on it.

It's essential to understand the role of the Introduction. It is designed to give a brief and summarized overview and not an extended presentation, the Introduction is used during a first meeting or at a networking event in front of other participants.

The most crucial part of networking is maintaining rapport to continue building the relationship. A good Introduction can generate increased interest in continuing the relationship, while a poor one can create distance, cause confusion, and result in a lack of interest.

When people ask, "What do you do?" they aren't asking because they want to know everything about what you do. In most cases, they are just starting the conversation.

> A GOOD INTRODUCTION CAN GENERATE INCREASED INTEREST IN CONTINUING THE RELATIONSHIP, WHILE A POOR ONE CAN CREATE DISTANCE, CAUSE CONFUSION, AND RESULT IN A LACK OF INTEREST.

As mentioned earlier, many people create a canned introduction. It is a good starting point, but this chapter will take it to a new level.

By the time you have finished this chapter, you will have the confidence to deliver your Introduction in front of any group at any time and have them wanting to connect with you afterward to continue the conversation.

We will accomplish this by helping you create a "Modular Introduction." We can break it into flexible sections that can easily be added or subtracted to fit your needs.

Let's start with your basic introduction. Your basic introduction will include your name, your profession, the products or services you provide, who your audience is that you serve, and the results you provide to them.

If you haven't ever played the game "Mad Libs," it is a book with fill-in-the-blank spots. After you ask your friend to fill in the blank with a noun, verb, pronoun, or whatever is called for, a funny paragraph or story would be the result.

To make it easy to simplify creating your Introduction, we will follow a similar process here. Consider taking out an additional paper and a pen or open the word processing program on your computer and follow along. After completing several variations, you will find the ones you love! Memorize the ones which convey the message you want to get across in a concise amount of time.

Creating your Standard Introduction

Here's the formula for your Standard Introduction:

My name is **(Name)** of **(Business Name)**.
I am a **(Title, Position, Role)**.
Who helps **(Your typical clients)**.
To **(What you help them accomplish, a result you help them get)**.
So that **(Main benefit they are looking for)**.

Examples:

If I am promoting my Networking Training business

My name is Chris Borja of "Become a Better Networker."
I am a Business Networking Consultant, Author, and Speaker
Who helps business professionals
To become confident and competent networkers
So that they can increase their revenue, reduce the amount of time prospecting, and make a more significant impact on their communities.

If I am promoting my Virtual Events Business

My name is Chris Borja of Borja Virtual, LLC
I am the CEO of a Virtual and Hybrid Event Production Company
That helps Non-Profit Organizations, Companies, and Conference Organizers

To create fun, engaging, and revenue-producing events So that they can make a more significant impact while building momentum and strengthening their community

As you can see, this is a great starting point. If you don't already have your Standard Introduction created, work on that now. Fill in the blanks and see which ones you like the best.

You may go through several variations until you find the one you like. Practice them by recording yourself, sharing them with friends you trust, and in real-life scenarios.

It's recommended that you continue refining this until you find the one that you love.

Creating your Modular Introduction

Remember, the problem with "canned" introductions is that they are not optimized for a specific audience. They are either too broad, too detailed, or irrelevant to those present.

You can adjust a Modular Introduction to fit any audience!

For example, suppose you are a Realtor sharing your introduction in front of College Seniors. In that case, you should share something different than your introduction in front of Senior Citizens!

In front of the College Seniors, you may want to include that you help first-time buyers purchase their new homes.

In front of the Senior Citizens, you may want to include that you help empty nesters with downsizing their homes.

You see how sharing that you help first-time home buyers would appeal to College, Seniors, and sharing that you help empty nesters would be appealing to Senior Citizens.

The reverse is true as well. College Seniors wouldn't care about downsizing because it is irrelevant to them. Senior Citizens probably wouldn't care that you help first-time home buyers because they are likely at a different stage of life.

By tailoring your introduction, it becomes relevant and much more interesting.

The formulas for your Modular Introduction are designed to fit the varying number of times that you have to give your introduction and fit the audience you are speaking to.

Here are the three different formats for your Modular Introduction:

Short – 1 to 3 words, approximately 5 seconds

Standard – 1 to 3 sentences, approximately 30-60 seconds

Extended – 1 to 3 short paragraphs, approximately 1 minute to 5 minutes+

What you include will be based on the amount of time that you have. We've all been to an event where somebody spoke too long and took up too much time giving their introduction. They are usually poorly prepared, wasting time sharing their background and irrelevant facts or stories. When this happens, many of the other participants subconsciously form a dislike for that person, which is not a good start!

Being concise and on point shows that you are clear and confident about who you can help and how you can help them, grabbing peoples' attention and making you more memorable. Those intrigued by your Modular Introduction will likely reach out to get to know you better.

Here's an important note regarding your Introduction. It's not just about what you say, it's about what they hear, what they understand, what they remember, and what they can repeat!

Let's start by getting the short version of your Modular Introduction down.

This ranges from 1 to 3 words and is typically less than 5 seconds. When you have this little time, it's because you are part of a large group, and there is a limited amount of time for introductions.

> IT'S NOT JUST ABOUT WHAT YOU SAY, IT'S ABOUT WHAT THEY HEAR, WHAT THEY UNDERSTAND, WHAT THEY REMEMBER, AND WHAT THEY CAN REPEAT!

Don't be the one that talks for a minute when everyone else has stuck to their time frame. You will not be favorably looked upon by others in the group.

Be clear and concise.

Short Modular Formula– 1 to 3 words, approximately 5 seconds

What would you say if someone asked you who you are and what you do?

Answer: My name is **(Name)** and I am a **(Title, Position, Role)**.

Ie. CPA, lawyer, investment manager, insurance broker, realtor, graduating student, editor, etc.

If you are struggling with how to fill in the blanks on any of your introductions, revisit the 20 questions for clarity in chapter 1.

Standard Modular Formula – 1 to 3 sentences, approximately 30-60 seconds

Since you already created a Standard Introduction earlier, we will use a different formula to make your Modular Introduction more effective! For this Modular Introduction, you will adapt what you say based on your audience and what they will find relatable.

Here is the formula for the Standard Modular Introduction:

Hi, my name is **(Name)** and I am a **(Title, Position, Role)** with **(Company name)**.

Share 2 to 3 problems/facts that your audience would relate to.
Problem/Fact #1
Problem/Fact #2
Problem/Fact #3 (optional)

So, what I/we do is:
Solution #1
Solution #2
Solution #3 (optional)

Close with a Call to Action (aka CTA) (If appropriate). This is your "ask" or desired response from your audience.

Expanding on the example we shared above with the realtor giving their introduction in front of college seniors, it might sound something like this:

Example #1 Realtor in front of College Seniors

Hi, my name is Rhonda, and I am a realtor with XYZ Realty Co.

We all know that buying your first house can be frightening and intimidating. Many first-time buyers worry about whether they can afford the home and what a good neighborhood to move into is, and the required paperwork can scare them off!

I help my first-time home buyers by educating them on the process, providing reports and insights about different neighborhoods, and holding their hand every step of the way until I hand them the keys to their new home.

If you know of any first-time home buyers, refer them to me, and I will be happy to help! Again, I'm Rhonda with XYZ Realty.

Example #2 Realtor in front of Senior Citizens

Hi, my name is Rhonda, and I am a realtor with XYZ Realty Co.

For most people raising a family, we look for a house with enough bedrooms to fit growing kids, enough bathrooms to not have a line in the hallway, and a yard for the kids to invite their friends and play with the family pet.

When the kids move out, empty nesters often find that they have too much space! Going up and down stairs may become a challenge, heating and cooling costs can be high for a mostly empty house and keeping the whole place clean is another story.

I help empty nesters find the perfect place for their new chapter in life while reducing monthly costs and hopefully putting some money in their pockets too! I also introduce them to my partners to help make the downsizing and moving hassle-free!

If you know of any empty nesters or future empty nesters, refer them to me. Again, I'm Rhonda with XYZ Realty, and I'd be happy to help!

Example #3 Auto Repair Shop Owner in front of Automobile Owners

Hi, my name is Scott. I am the owner of Scott's Automotive Repair.

Most people love their cars until it makes that weird noise, needs costly service, or just decides not to start one morning when they have an important meeting.

Unfortunately, mechanics have received a bad rap based on bad experiences, getting overcharged, or having the same problem reoccur after taking the car home.

What I do is I use my ten years of experience along with the latest training and technology to diagnose the issue accurately, provide my clients with an accurate estimate, and educate them on their cars' problems and the repairs that address those problems.

I provide everything in writing and even show them the replaced parts along with pictures to give them confidence in the repairs made and the reliability of their car.

If you know anyone with car issues, send them my way, and I'll take good care of them. My name is Scott of Scott's Automotive Repair.

I hope you find these examples helpful.

Now it's time for you to create your Modular Introduction. To make it easier for you to come up with the problems and facts that your audience will relate to, take a moment to put yourself in their shoes. In the example above, you can see how tailoring the issues we solve for our audience can make a big difference for that realtor or auto mechanic.

Take some time right now to draft different versions of your Modular Introduction. Begin the process with your audience being a mix of diverse business professionals. Then create different versions for other audiences that you may be speaking with.

Remember that this doesn't just apply to large audiences. This Modular Introduction can be adapted for individuals you are meeting for the first time. With this new skill of quickly adapting your introduction to fit your audience, it's essential to understand who you are talking to whenever possible. We will go into this skill in greater depth in the upcoming chapter on "Working Events."

Practice your different versions on camera and in front of friends. Practice real-life interactions.

Don't expect to get it perfect the first time. Keep on practicing.

Observe your audiences' reactions and see if your words resonate with them. A good sign that your Introduction is resonating with them, is when they subconsciously nod their heads as you share the "problems and facts that they can relate to."

Make adjustments until you get the response that you are looking for. Practice this formula with different audiences in mind until it becomes second nature, and you can create a Modular Introduction that fits any situation, on the spot!

Extended – 1 to 3 short paragraphs, approximately 1 min. to 5 min.+

When you have more time available for your introduction, avoid the trap of going deeper into explaining your products or services. This usually leads to overwhelm, potential confusion, and reduced interest in another meeting to learn more.

Instead, add 1 or 2 relevant success stories or testimonials to paint a better picture of what you do. These are powerful because the human mind remembers stories more than facts.

Gather testimonials and stories for an Extended Modular Introduction. Write down at least one story to match each variation of the problem/solution.

Now you know exactly what to say when networking or meeting new people! This one skill will give you tons of confidence and improve your results as you begin many new relationships!

Chapter 15

Creating Your Business Cards and Website

This chapter will help you establish some critical components to building your brand. While your brand is much bigger than your business card, flyers, or website, they play a role in the big picture.

One of the things that makes people feel less confident is needing to prepare for an opportunity. For example, when I meet somebody, and we get to the end of the conversation where it's time to exchange contact information, and I ask for their business card if they don't have one, the look on their face is one of embarrassment. They usually make excuses like, "Oh, I need to update them." "I need to make new ones." Or maybe they have some old cards, and they need to cross out the old information and handwrite the new information.

Being prepared will increase your confidence. Creating materials that you are proud of and represent you well will make you all the more eager to make more connections and have the opportunity to share your brand and message with them.

Marketing collateral is anything you can use to promote your company's brand or message. This can include material such as business cards, flyers, brochures, and posters. This can include blog posts, ebooks, case studies, and videos.

We won't cover all of these in this chapter. Instead, we will focus on the basics to launch you into your networking journey.

Let's start with your business cards. Networking isn't just swapping business cards or passing out as many of them as possible. But they do have a place.

A nice quality business card that stands out and represents you, your company, and your brand can play a role in making a good first impression and being remembered.

Whether you design your own business cards or have somebody do it for you, it's important to make them visually appealing and eye-catching.

Could you just use a basic white card with your name, phone number, and email? Sure, you could! It'll get the job done by sharing your basic contact information.

But why not maximize your opportunity to build your brand with the same effort? Clarifying who you serve and how you provide value will play a role in the design of your business cards.

With modern technology, there are so many options to make your cards stand out. They may cost more than your standard white business cards with plain text, but they will pay many dividends.

They will help you stand out at the event. It can add an additional conversation topic, depending on what you do with your card. It will make you more memorable to the person you just met after some time has passed, and your card sits in a stack of other business cards in their desk drawer.

So how do you make your cards stand out? Here are some ideas.

If you are in a field where you can display your work visually, consider going with a full-color business card. You can include an image of yourself or something that represents your work at-a-glance. Your card will have all your standard information like name, website, email, and phone number. Also, consider including a tagline or slogan that helps you be memorable.

You can also utilize the back side of the card. Most people only use the front because they aren't aware of how to use the back side or don't want to spend a few extra dollars.

The back side of your business card can also be displayed in full color if that makes sense for your business. Other options to maximize the back of your business card are putting an appointment reminder on the back or, depending on your business or industry, you can put something on the back that makes it worth keeping on an ongoing basis.

It could be a calendar, a schedule of upcoming events, a QR code that leads to your website or video presentation, or any other link of your choice. You could add a restaurant tip calculator, a frequent customer rewards form, or a sports team schedule.

Another idea to make your business card stand out is the selective use of foil. This can add an excellent highlight or accent to your business card and make it look elegant and high-class. This would be a nice touch, especially if you offer high-ticket items or services. Again, this is part of creating your brand.

New technology has allowed some unique styles of business cards, like cards laser cut on metal. You can also have a card made of semi-transparent plastic. Cards can be made with multiple layers and colors, adding thickness while enhancing the design.

Another is to place a stick-on magnet on the back so your new connections can put it on their refrigerator or file cabinet and use it to hold other papers up.

Adding a magnet on the back of your business card is my favorite. After visiting my in-laws in California, I got the idea when I saw several realtor business cards on the refrigerator. I asked my wife if she knew who they were. She said she didn't, but they had been there forever.

Her parents used the business cards magnets to hold their grocery lists, to-do lists, and photos. I thought, "What a great way to advertise!" Free impressions every day!

You can purchase these magnets at an office supply store, Amazon, or eBay. You'll get your best deals online. They are called "Self-Adhesive Business Card Magnets." You simply peel the back and stick it on your card!

This will give you the most options for your business card design while still being magnetic.

You can order magnetic business cards directly from your printer, but typically they have fewer options on the design.

After I began using these magnetic business cards, I noticed a few things. I was proud of these and happy to give them out as I met people. Two, the person I hand them to instantly notices the added thickness and weight of the card, making it feel more substantial. Three, I usually get a compliment, and it becomes an additional conversation topic. Four, I've had people tell me they knew exactly where they would place it in their office.

I met somebody at training, and after talking for a few minutes, she said, "I feel like I know you from somewhere." After spending a few more minutes trying to figure it out, she had the light bulb go on. Her eyes widened, and she excitedly said, "That's where I know you from! Your business card is on my refrigerator!

My roommate attended one of your events a few years ago. She placed your business card on our fridge, and it's still there!"

So, I think they work great and are a wonderful investment.

Take the time to design them, convey the message you want to get across, be willing to invest a little bit more to get a quality product, and make this a productive tool in your networking activities.

We live in a rapidly advancing technological age that changes how we do business. Some vendors and apps allow you to design a digital business card with all of your standard contact information but with added links to your social media profiles, presentations, and calendar app to book appointments on the spot.

These digital business cards are easy to share through your phone by forwarding a link via email or text or even by having someone scan your QR code on their phone. If you do an online search under "Digital Business Card," you will find several different vendors. Pick one that fits your needs, create a card design that fits your brand, update all of your relevant information, and you'll never be without a business card when you need one!

Next, let's talk about your website. If you already have one, then you are all set! If you don't have one, I would recommend creating a basic site to get you started. I say this because it looks more professional on your collateral, making it easy for you to share your business, your message, and your brand by simply sharing a link.

If you have the ability to hire someone to design your website, then do it! Ensure they include all of the information from step one of this book.

If you don't have a website because you are just getting started, or you don't have an updated one to fit your current goals and branding, you can quickly create a landing page using drag-and-drop software by searching for "do-it-yourself website builder."

On your website, use professional images of yourself and your work. If you don't have any images or are working on them now, you can do an online search for "free stock photos" to get started.

The critical components of your website are **About, Products and Services**, and **Contact**. These are just the basics to get you started. Take the time and invest in having this represent you and your brand.

Next, we will look at utilizing social media to build your network and brand.

Chapter 16

Social Media: Pick Your Major, Your Minor, and Your Electives

If you are an avid social media user, these next few chapters will take you to the next level and remind you of the fundamentals required to grow your network intentionally. If you are new to social media, we will walk you through the basics and cover the strategies for using social media effectively.

Social media is supposed to be "social." Unfortunately, when most people start using social media for business purposes, they forget that it is SOCIAL media, not "spam everyone about my business" media!

Several different platforms are available nowadays. Most certainly, new ones will develop while others will disappear forever. Each platform has a different audience and manner of reaching that audience.

For someone new to the social media world, and even for frequent users, being active and having a presence on every platform is impossible! There are way too many to keep up with.

Posting is one thing, but creating meaningful engagement and building intentional relationships is a whole other thing.

After completing high school, students who decide to continue on their educational path in college are met with the overwhelming decision of picking their major. It's a tough decision because they are often forced to choose from a list and lack practical experience with those majors.

There are some parallels between selecting a college major and choosing which social media platforms you will invest your time in. I suggest spending some time using the different platforms and exploring how they can be beneficial to building your brand, your network, and your business.

Maintaining a presence and advancing your goals through social media should be fun. The way I look at social media is that it's an extension of real conversations with real people. These conversations lead to genuine relationships that build trust and unlimited possibilities for growth, no matter which platform you decide on. So, try them out and pick your major, minor, and electives!

My major would be LinkedIn, my minor would be Facebook, and my electives would be Instagram and TikTok™. For you, that may look a little bit different.

Regardless of which ones you choose, remember to pick one major, one minor, and however many electives you are interested in.

For your major, this is where you will spend the most significant percentage of your time on social media. This is where you have the best opportunity to reach your target market and build relationships for referrals and potential partnerships. You will post once a day and engage with others regularly.

For your minor, you will spend about half as much time as you spend on your major but will have the same goals and activities as above.

For your electives, you can do whatever you like. You can use it for fun, entertainment, and occasional business contacts from time to time.

Instagram is my elective platform. I have pages for business, but I also have pages for personal hobbies where I can connect with others with similar interests.

One of the reasons why social media works well is because it helps to build trust. As a general observation, we tend to trust people we know more about and distrust people we don't know much about.

Think about the saying, "I don't know about that guy." It usually refers to somebody that you don't trust.

Social media is an opportunity to be seen and build trust even before conversing with someone. For example, if you just met somebody and connected with them on social media, you would likely want to know a little more about them and scroll through their posts and pictures. If we do that with others we meet, we can safely assume they do the same and look into our profiles.

SOCIAL MEDIA IS AN OPPORTUNITY TO BE SEEN AND BUILD TRUST EVEN BEFORE CONVERSING WITH SOMEONE.

So, as we look at our new connections' profiles, we may see that they enjoy family time, perhaps do some volunteer work in their community, and maybe have a hobby or two that we share. Perhaps they've traveled to places we would like to go or places we've been to. We may find that we share common favorite foods or fitness activities. We might even learn a little more about their business within their profile!

People frequently overlook the actual value of networking on social media because they think of it as a way to promote their business instead of building their personal brand, which includes all aspects of their life, and who they are as a person.

All of us have competitors, and one of the goals in marketing is to differentiate ourselves from our competitors. One of the best ways to differentiate yourself is through the relationship and trust you build with others. Social media provides the opportunity for you to be more visible, stay top of mind, and be someone they trust.

Some people see social media as being time-consuming. In some ways, they are correct. But the way I see it, social media provides us with a way to stay in contact with hundreds or even thousands of people on a daily basis! Imagine the old days when staying in touch required making a phone call or sending a letter. That would be time-consuming!

Viewing every post and comment as a "micro-conversation" helps me appreciate this modern-day technology's value.

I hope you begin to see the value and leverage social media to help you conveniently grow genuine relationships from anywhere in the world!

Chapter 17

How to Use LinkedIn™

LinkedIn is one of the best and most underutilized networking tools available.

When I started my networking journey in 2012, I had no LinkedIn presence. I had an account. However, I didn't utilize it and often thought all LinkedIn email alerts were SPAM!

A friend of mine asked if I was using LinkedIn and when I said no, he was shocked! He asked me who I was interested in meeting, and at the time, I was looking to connect with small business owners. He showed me how I could instantly access small business owners in Columbus, Ohio, with the "advanced search" feature.

He had my attention.

When I got home, I tried to log in and didn't even know what email I had set up the account under. I did the whole, "forgot password" thing and logged in. I had about 120 connections, of whom I had no clue who they were.

Instead of trying to salvage this account, I started a new one from scratch. LinkedIn allows you to sync your existing contacts when creating a new account. You can select all or choose specific contacts by clicking on their check box. This is a fast way to add to your LinkedIn connections.

In this chapter, I will share the fundamentals to help you start your LinkedIn journey.

Step one is to create your LinkedIn profile. This begins with your name. Make sure you use your proper name and one that people can use to find you through a search. You can hyphenate or put the name in parentheses if you have multiple names or changed names for any reason.

Do not use additional characters like asterisks or other signs that could affect your ability to be found in searches. Also, do not put additional slogans, tag lines, websites, phone numbers, or links as part of your name.

Select a profile picture that represents you and your brand. Your photo does not need to be taken by a professional photographer, but it does need to be a professional-looking photo.

Make sure it shows your face clearly with good lighting and a clean background. Do not put pictures of your logo, your dog, your cat, your favorite sports team, or a photo from a party with your ex cropped out!

Now it's time to select a cover photo. This large image will appear at the top of your profile on mobile and web versions of the platform. Since this is a prominent image, use this valuable real estate wisely.

Some ideas for this space are using it to display your logo, your business location, or pictures of the products or services you offer! Use a design that represents your brand. You can create it yourself or have someone design and create it for you. As the saying goes, a picture is worth a thousand words! Take full advantage of it!

For your headline, choose your words carefully and be intentional. On LinkedIn, your headline appears next to your name, and everywhere you post or comment.

This feature does not occur on any other social media platform.

Think about what you want everyone to know about you. Now, convey that in just a few short words. This can change as you evolve and grow and become more familiar with how you will be using LinkedIn. I would suggest that your headline is geared towards appealing to the ideal audience that you wrote down in step one of this book.

You can put several different titles for your headline, but only the first few words will appear. Put the most important ones at the front of your headline. My current headline reads: "Community-Builder | Business Networking Consultant, Speaker, and Coach | Virtual and Hybrid Events Specialist | Publisher."

This represents all of my current companies. The first few words in my headline were intentionally selected because when my name shows up, I want people to see that I am a community builder. This is more universally appealing from a networking standpoint as I engage and make new connections throughout the platform.

During the pandemic, I had the Virtual and Hybrid Events title positioned first on my headline because that was the primary networking focus during a time when face-to-face meetings were not possible.

Post-pandemic, I didn't feel like it was something that most people would find a need to connect with me if they weren't actively looking for someone to help them with an event, so I changed the headline to the one mentioned earlier.

Another way to use the headline is to put a small piece of your Modular Introduction to capture attention. You'll notice that everything we work on in this book is a building block for something to follow.

Whether LinkedIn is your major, minor, or elective, this is the one social media platform that I think is non-negotiable from a networking standpoint.

Your LinkedIn "about" section is next. Many people use this section to "sell" their products or services. I would recommend that you utilize this space to help people get to know you as a person. There is plenty of opportunity for you to share about your products and services in the experience section, which we will cover shortly.

Here are some ideas you can include in your about section. Make it anywhere from one to three paragraphs. Start with who you are and some of your interests. You can share things about where you live, grew up, your family, and any interesting hobbies. You can even share a little bit about your pets! I suggest writing in 1st person rather than 3rd person to create a stronger connection with the viewer.

All of these personal elements humanize you. It also displays potential connection points between you and them. These connection points help build relationships faster than your company or business descriptions would.

Next, share a little bit of your professional background and how you got to where you are now. Share your passion for what you do now and why it's important. Finish with your current profession or business.

Close with a statement that encourages someone to feel comfortable connecting with you. You can say, "I'm always open to new connections and seeing how we can help one another."

For the experience section, you will list all of your relevant jobs and businesses. You do not need to put every single position you've held for the last twenty years (unless you want to). For example, I was helping a real estate investor update her profile. She had a job listed over 25 years ago as a nail technician.

There is nothing wrong with listing that, but you can see how her nail technician job is not relevant 25 years later to her current career as a real estate investor. If you are looking for a job, you should list all relevant experiences on your LinkedIn experience section like you would list them on your job resume.

If you held some exciting positions in the past, you might want to include them simply because it is a conversation topic. Use your best judgment here on what to include and what not to include.

In the experience section, search your official company name so that you are listed as an employee of that company on LinkedIn, providing others with an additional link to find you.

If you own your own company, you will want to start a business page on LinkedIn to create a business profile and include your logo so that your company and your logo appear under the experience section.

You can have several different listings in the experience section for each role you've held over the years. In the description of each position, you can list your sales copy if you offer products, services, or goods.

If you are looking for employment, use the description of each role to highlight your accomplishments, skills, and qualities that would make you appealing to potential employers.

If you run a non-profit, association, or organization, you can use this space to share your mission, the impact you're making, and also any requests of who you are looking to connect with.

Over the last few years, LinkedIn has added some nice features to the experience section. You can now add a website link, photos, resume, presentation, or even a link to your landing page.

More sections help you connect with other users. You can add your education and connect with fellow alumni. You can also add any volunteering that you do, which helps highlight the organization you support and connects you with other volunteers.

Another benefit of using LinkedIn is building trust through "Social Proof." The two sections that help you with your social proof are the skills section and the recommendation section.

For the skills section, I recommend you put skills relevant to your current goals. Avoid selecting too many skills because it makes it more challenging to show your expertise in an area that counts the most. Fellow LinkedIn users can endorse you for the skills that you select. The higher number of endorsements, the more credible you become.

You can display LinkedIn's version of reviews and testimonials in the recommendation section. LinkedIn users can select their relationship with you and write a recommendation that helps to build your trust and credibility.

The last section that we cover is Interests. In this section of your profile, you can select influencers and leaders in your field, industry, or a topic you have a personal interest in so that you can follow them any time they post. Engaging with these influencers will allow you to build your network with others who have similar interests.

By completing all of your LinkedIn sections, you will receive a status called "LinkedIn All-Star." This means that you have a complete profile, and LinkedIn is more likely to show your profile to others as they search. Following these steps will help you to fully utilize this platform to grow your networking brand and accomplish your goals.

If you need help with your LinkedIn, go to www.networkingessentialsforsuccess.com/linkedin for additional training and resources.

Chapter 18

How to Use Facebook™

This book includes this training on Facebook (rebranded as META™) because it is still the number one social media platform. Sure, many people complain about Facebook and its algorithm and privacy policies, censorship, and invasive advertising, but the funny thing is that most people complain about Facebook on Facebook!

From a networking standpoint, Facebook is a great tool. I like to use LinkedIn and Facebook in combination whenever possible. LinkedIn provides a professional profile, and Facebook spotlights more of who the person is behind the business.

As stated in an earlier chapter, the more we know about somebody, the more we trust them. The less we know about somebody, the less we trust them. In this chapter, I will share some strategies and best practices for building quality relationships through this platform. I will share some tips on what you should and should not do.

Most of you reading this already have a Facebook profile. If you want to separate your business and personal connections, I suggest creating a second personal profile and a business page.

I started off being super private on Facebook and limited my connections only to close family and friends. Over time, I started becoming friends with more and more of my business contacts, and slowly it became much more public.

For those concerned about privacy, I recommend being selective with what you post and only sharing things that you are ok with the world knowing. We live in a digital age, and this advice applies to everything we do online, including text messages and emails.

When we meet somebody new, whether in a networking or a personal context, and we want to know more about them, our first tendency is to go to social media to look them up! It happens if you want to hire somebody for your company and want to see what they are about. It occurs if somebody is looking to do business with you. It even happens on a personal level if your best friend is dating somebody new, and you want to check out their new love interest to see if you trust them!

If we were to look at your Facebook profile this very minute, what impression would we have of you? Would it be the brand that you want to build? Or would it show something else? Are you someone that would appear to be trustworthy or someone we should be cautious about?

We all make rapid decisions about whether or not we like or trust somebody. This all happens in our subconscious minds. What we display on social media registers in the viewers' minds

Now that we know that our social media profiles play a big role in our brand, let me share some best practices on using Facebook in building your network effectively.

> WE ALL MAKE RAPID DECISIONS ABOUT WHETHER OR NOT WE LIKE OR TRUST SOMEBODY.

Keep it social. People do not want to see your business pitches every day. If you've done that in the past, stop it now. It does not work!

What does work, however, is having real conversations through your posts and also their posts. Engagement is the key. While some people feel like social media wastes time, it depends on how you use it. If you are simply consuming content, gossiping, and spewing negativity into the world, then yes, it is a waste of time.

On the other hand, if you realize that there are real people at the other end of that profile, you can have dozens of significant conversations, quickly building rapport and relationships!

I look at all my interactions on Facebook as "micro-conversations." To me, it's just like sending a text message, except it's public and more people can join the conversation.

The significance of this as a networker is that you get to be top of mind which is helpful when somebody needs your services. The cool part is that you don't need to keep promoting your business to stay top of mind.

Most people will know what you do if you share your business about 5% of the time on social media. The key now is to stay visible. Facebook is a great way to stay visible while spreading love, joy, encouragement, support, and positivity (at least if you choose to do so).

I started networking back in 2012. It was at that time that I started using Facebook intentionally. Whenever

I met someone new in person, if we had a good connection and wanted to stay in touch, I would ask them if they were on Facebook. We would connect and stay in touch through that platform if they were.

For many of the people I met, we didn't end up meeting for lunch or seeing each other again, in many cases, for years! But because of our Facebook connection, we could stay in touch with each other's lives as we shifted, adapted, and grew through the years.

Many people have reached out to me after years of not talking face-to-face and becoming clients. I met a gentleman several years ago at one of our luncheons with whom we primarily stayed in touch through our Facebook pages.

Recently we reconnected as our networking group was expanding into his city. We are now partnered in developing that new city together. This is the power of staying connected through Facebook!

Many Facebook strategies are available to help you grow, including business pages and advertising. As a tool for networking, however, look at Facebook as another method of staying in touch daily, creating trust and rapport, and keeping you top of mind.

Chapter 19

Other Social Media Platforms

One of the main considerations to determine which platforms you should use is whether your audience is on that platform. Depending on your business or networking goals, some platforms may work better than others.

Establishing your major, your minor, and your electives is a good way to create order and avoid being overwhelmed by trying to be present on every platform available.

I fell into the trap of chasing the next best thing every time a new platform came out, trying to be one of the "early adopters" and building a huge following on that platform. I paid lots of money investing in different programs and systems, of which none worked for me.

I believe they didn't work because the strategies were designed to draw in a bunch of strangers who had no clue who I was. It also relied on each platform's algorithms to show my content on my followers' news feeds, which was a very small percentage.

I'm not saying that these social media strategies do not work. Some people have made millions of dollars through their social media following. These strategies didn't work for me because these platforms continue to evolve, and what works today becomes quickly outdated.

Do you know what always remains relevant? Building genuine relationships with real people!

So, when I talk about using these social media platforms, the focus is on connecting with individuals instead of blanketing the masses and hoping for the best.

All these platforms are just another vehicle to communicate with people. Let's explore some of these platforms and give you an idea of what would be a good fit for what you are hoping to accomplish.

The real goal is to turn online relationships into in-person connections and vice versa. Relationships lead to influence which leads to opportunities!

I won't go into much detail on the various social platforms in this chapter because the goal is to share a brief overview so you can identify what might work best for you and not provide full training on each social media platform. There's plenty of online information available that will be a better resource since things in the world of social media change fast!

Here's a brief overview of what each platform may work best for. Take a look, check them out, and make an educated decision for yourself and your business. If you change your mind, no worries! Remember, the platform is just a vehicle to create more connections and build relationships.

Instagram would work great for image-oriented businesses or brands. Since the platform mainly focuses on photos and videos, it lends itself well to industries that rely on visuals. This includes photographers, videographers, fashion designers, lifestyle coaches, fitness and health experts, travel agents, artists, and many more.

Twitter™ is focused mainly on stories, events, and news. It's a great place to see what's trending and what's hot in the news. You can follow influencers or companies to see what's happening in real-time.

Pinterest™ is a great place to share posts that inspire creativity and share images and content that you find interesting. Pinterest would be a good fit for those into crafting and building projects and those interested in sharing ideas on design, fashion, and trends, to name a few.

TikTok is the newest platform and fastest growing, with primarily a younger audience. But that is slowly changing. This is the platform to be on to reach the younger generation. It is mainly for fun, but if you can share your business without being too formal and business-like, you can reach your potential audiences.

YouTube™ is also something to consider even though it's often overlooked as a social media platform. YouTube is a great place to create your own channel, share your expertise, and take advantage of the fact that it is the #2 search engine behind Google™!

I have an account on each social media platform, but I don't spend much time on them. I check on them occasionally just to see what's happening. Since these fall under my electives category, I view these more for fun and leisure.

This helps to avoid overwhelm in trying to grow my business on every platform. I know that my major is LinkedIn. My minor is Facebook™. These other social media platforms are my electives.

Your major, minor, and electives will differ based on your business, audience, and goals. I hope this helps you prioritize what makes the most sense for achieving your goals while keeping the "social" in social media!

Chapter 20

Calendar Management and Contact Management Systems

Growing your network will require you to get more organized than ever. In the old days, growing a sizable network would require a good assistant to manage your appointments and all your new contacts. While some of you already have this person in place, I know many of you do not.

Fortunately, technological advances can make the organization of your growing network a breeze. In this chapter, I will share a few strategies and tools to help you create stronger relationships in a shorter time.

Everyone has a different preference when it comes to managing their calendar. Some people prefer a paper calendar that they can physically write on, while others have gone paperless, utilizing digital calendars 100%. A third group has adopted neither of these and has no type of calendar management whatsoever.

The main thing is to use a system that works for you!

Your calendar is the primary way to budget and properly allocate your time. We all have the same 24 hours in a day. Poorly managing your calendar, or not managing it at all, will leave you saying things like, "I don't have time for working out." "I don't have time to meet for coffee." "I don't have time to go to that networking event." "I don't have time to watch my kids' ballgame." "I don't have time to go on a date with my significant other."

The way I plan my calendar is by starting with the significant events. These are the events that you know you aren't missing. Significant events might be your best friends' wedding, an annual conference, a one-week vacation to Florida, or a child's graduation!

Notice how you don't miss significant events! It just doesn't happen!

That means you can make the time if something is important to you! So, let's go back to calendar management. My calendar begins with booking all of these significant events first. Once they are on my calendar, there is no chance I am missing them outside of some type of emergency.

The next time you say, "I don't have time for date night, or my kids' game, or working out, etc." add this to the end of your sentence... "because it's not a priority." Let that soak in for a minute.

How does it feel to say that? The reality is that we have the time for things that are important to us and the things that we want to do.

I remember seeing a funny T-shirt with bold letters that said, "Sorry I'm late. I didn't want to come."

What does this have to do with networking? If you don't have the right mindset, you will likely find a convenient excuse not to do the activity that will change your business, life, and community.

Just like a computer network requires every part of the circuit to be connected, we play a critical role as a connector in our community.

Your calendar is where you designate time for these connections, whether meeting with an individual or in a large group setting.

Here is a simple system that you can use to manage your calendar. Start with the important things as we described above. Schedule your events and meetings 90 days in advance. Schedule your family time and your "you" time. Now that you have scheduled those, you need to create time to grow your network!

Coordinating an available time and date is challenging enough for one person. It becomes even more challenging for each additional person it needs to work for. What happens in the networking world is the lack of knowledge of modern technology that can eliminate the back and forth of finding a convenient time to meet.

Here is an example of a typical dialog between Tom and Sue, trying to schedule a meeting:

Tom: "Hey Sue, it was great meeting you. I look forward to connecting to learn more about your business!"

Sue: "That'll be great! I look forward to it, and I look forward to learning more about yours as well!"

Tom: "What's the best time and date for you?"

Sue: "Friday's usually work best for me either before 10 am or after 3 pm."

Tom: "Fridays are not good for me. I'm typically in planning meetings all day Friday."

Sue: "What typically works best for you?"

Tom: "It varies depending on the week. I just need to know in advance."

Sue: "How about next Tuesday at 2 pm?"

Tom: "Normally that would be good, except next Tuesday I'll be out of town."

OK, I can go on, but you get the point. You've probably experienced this. It becomes so much effort that often meetings just don't happen! Imagine all of the lost opportunities that result from this type of inefficiency!

I recommend that you get an electronic scheduling app. This will save you time while making you look like an absolute pro! Here's what that same conversation would look like if Tom had a scheduling app:

Tom: "Hey Sue, it was great meeting you. I look forward to connecting to learn more about your business!"

Sue: "That'll be great! I look forward to it, and I look forward to learning more about yours as well!"

Tom: "Let's make it happen! Do you have a scheduling app, or do you want me to send you my link?"

Sue: "No, I don't have one. Send me your link."

Tom: [texts link to Sue]

Sue: "Got it! Booked with you for next Wednesday at 11:30 a.m.!"

Tom: "Awesome! See you then!"

The scheduling app will add the appointment to Tom's and Sue's calendars and send them reminder emails with customizable messages. This means forgotten appointments and no-shows become a thing of the past! Oh, and you know those last-minute things that pop up, and someone needs to reschedule? They can do that directly on the electronic calendar and find an alternate time on the spot!

Some examples of electronic scheduling apps include Calendly, Acuity, and Hubspot, to name a few. Use a scheduling app that links with your phone's calendar to keep everything synchronized and avoid double-booking a time slot. Search for "Meeting Scheduler Apps," and you'll find dozens of choices and select the one that fits you best! I use Calendly and find it very helpful.

The next part of your organization is contact management software. This is also commonly known as CRM, Customer Relationship Management. You will find many software providers if you search for either of these terms. Many of them will be highly robust and much more than you need if you are just starting.

The most important thing about the CRM you decide to use is the one that is easiest for you to maintain and update. If it is too complex, chances are you will not utilize it to its fullest capabilities.

Your CRM is where you will keep track of all of your network's information. It is OK to take small steps and make adjustments when you are just getting started. In this section, I will share a straightforward way to keep track of your new connections.

For those who use a smartphone, you already have an effortless way to keep track of your new connections. Depending on your phone, you will have a version of "contacts." As you save each person's name, you can also include their email address, phone number, mailing address, birthday, social media profile, additional customizable fields, and the best part, notes!

One of the reasons I like your phone's native contacts app for new networkers is that you don't need to learn any new software. It's always on you, and you can message or call them with the touch of a button. Every time you make some type of contact with them, you can update your notes.

Keeping good notes is important because we will quickly forget details, even within minutes. Writing down notes is an excellent habit to have!

When I was ten, my parents would take me to the dentist. Every time I was there, the dentist would ask me how my last game was. She knew that I was a pitcher for my Little League baseball team. There's no way she could remember these details after seeing dozens of patients every day for several months between my visits.

The secret was in my file folder containing notes about my Little League pitching career. The fact that she had something to talk to me about while I sat in the chair made the visit less intimidating and much more pleasant.

Apply this example to your networking efforts. Imagine meeting somebody, and several months later, you run into each other again. Then they ask you about something you shared in that initial meeting. It may be a trip you went on, a project you were excited about, or something about your family. How do you feel about this person that remembered something that was important to you?

Either they have an incredible memory, or they have an excellent note-taking system. Whichever one of these two is true, you probably feel good about them and the fact that they listened to you. This is a learned skill which is good because it means that anyone can do it with some intentionality and practice.

Every week or two, I visit my chiropractor. By the time I get to the back, he has usually reviewed my electronic file on his computer. He knows what issues I had last time and typically has a conversation about something we discussed at the prior visit. Once I am done with my alignment, he is at his computer updating his notes as I pick up my things and get ready to head out the door.

He does this without fail for every single client that walks through his door! This allows him to have meaningful conversations with all his clients, creating an additional rapport that helps his business grow through retention and referrals.

Good contact management is a habit that you can begin today. Start simply by updating the contacts on your phone. Another simple tool already available on your phone is your "Notes" app. This is different from taking notes for each of your contacts.

Your Notes app is a blank digital sheet where you can jot down some notes. One of my strategies is to create a folder titled "Names." Within the Names folder, I will have notes named after places where I frequently meet people.

Some ideas for note names are networking group, gym, office, church, car club, company, events, conferences, neighbors, etc.

For example, if I met someone new at church who attended for the first time this Sunday, I would open the folder titled "church" and put the date that I met them, their name, and any relevant notes to help me remember them or something we talked about.

When I run into them again, I can quickly open my app and be reminded of their name and something we discussed. I don't take notes right in front of them. Instead, I would try to remember, and as soon as we finished our conversation, I would then go on my phone and update notes.

If I'm talking to many other people and don't have the opportunity to take notes on the spot, I will do my best to remember some bullet points and update my notes as soon as I get to the car.

This is an effective and straightforward way to keep track of your network as you start this journey. You can also use your notes app and create folders for prospects, for follow-up, or for introductions that you need to make.

As I said earlier, there are hundreds of CRM product solutions. Feel free to research and find one you like and one you will use.

Just a quick recap on this chapter. Get yourself organized. Save time by using an electronic meeting scheduler. Sync it with your calendar. Prioritize your events and activities. Create time for your networking and relationship-building activities.

If you are just starting your CRM, use the simple method I outlined above. If you are ready for something more robust, search online for various CRM options.

By having a solid foundation built on clarity (Step 1), a healthy mindset (Step 2), and your systems and tools (Step 3), you will have confidence and genuine excitement for meeting new people (Step 4)!

Step 4
Meet New People

Chapter 21

Finding the Time and Making Time

In the last chapter, we covered calendar management and prioritization. We make time for things we want to do that are essential to us. However, we don't always make time for things we should do.

For example, we should eat healthier, get enough sleep, drink enough water, exercise, and reach out to our loved ones. But we often don't do any of it regularly. If someone invited us last minute to a ballgame or a concert, we push other things off in order to go!

If networking is something that you SHOULD do, there is a good chance that something will get in the way. If it's not part of your habit or routine, there is a slim chance you will do what it takes to achieve your goals.

How can you shift your mindset, so you want to network as much as you want to go to the ballgame? For me, networking is a social activity as much as a business activity. I view it as more social than I do see it as a business. Strangely, I enjoy a networking event even more than a party because the engagement and the conversations are just as fun, except networking can lead to additional opportunities that parties generally don't.

As you shift your mindset and make networking a way of life, you will see that networking happens everywhere! It doesn't have to be an official networking event for networking to take place. It can happen on the sidelines of your daughter's soccer game, at your hiking club meeting, volunteer activity, or company lunch!

Some people have a misunderstanding of what networking is. They think that networking is a boring meeting where people try to sell each other stuff. If that is their understanding of networking, I can see why they would avoid it at all costs!

A better perspective of networking would be when we invest time to meet one another, build a relationship, learn about how we can provide for other's needs, and share resources that would be helpful. More often than not, those resources are not the exact product or services we offer. Those resources could be knowledge, advice, support, connections, finances, or encouragement.

Over the last ten years, I have made many lifelong friends. I have met more people in the last ten years than in my previous 40 years! More importantly, the connections made through introductions magnify the impact of our network.

When you adopt a healthy mindset about networking and recognize its potential to improve your life as you serve others in the community, finding the time to network no longer becomes a struggle. It's no longer something that you have to do. It's something that you get to do. It is one of the most rewarding ways of growing your business.

It allows you to grow exponentially because you now have a community of people who know you and want to introduce you to those who can use your products, services, or goods. Remember the big events we talked about in the last chapter? With the right mindset, your networking activities become those big events you don't want to miss. Your networking activities put time back on your schedule that you would otherwise have spent "prospecting."

Instead of chasing individual sales, you can now focus on creating bigger wins through collaboration. We will explore this more deeply in the later chapters.

Chapter 22

Different Types of Events and Networking Opportunities

Now that you have created time in your calendar to network, it's time to find some events. There are several places to find events that are happening near you.

Remember that we can also network anywhere people are gathering. It doesn't need to be an official networking event. You can network at your local cycling, hiking, or book club!

In this chapter, I will share an overview of the different types of events so that you can understand the benefits that each has.

Open-networking

Philosophy: Gathering people who want to meet others. It's generally a free-flowing event with minimal programming.

Pros:

- Freedom to meet everyone in the room, with maximum time for conversation.
- Fun reuniting with old friends
- Opportunity to meet many new people
- Freedom to spend more time, or less time with any given person
- Lack of structure can leave newer networkers feeling lost

Cons:

- Can get stuck listening to one person for too long
- No formal introductions in front of the room, resulting in less exposure to the group
- Not sure of what others do until starting the conversation
- A tendency for people who already know one another to gather and form cliques

Best practices:

- Arrive early to meet the organizer and leaders

- Ask if they need any help setting up
- Stay after the event ends! That's typically when the best connections are made.
- Be the connector at the event
- Invite others into your conversation
- Help the ones who look like they're lost
- Schedule extra time after the event and be the last one to leave
- Always thank the organizers and volunteers before leaving. You will be more memorable and leave a positive impression.

Referral Groups

Philosophy: Provide a structured group to build trust and share referrals. A typical group will have one representative per industry, i.e., one realtor, financial planner, insurance professional, auto mechanic, etc.

Pros:

- The intentional goal of giving and receiving referrals
- Structure and programming to make meetings efficient

- Requirement for members to attend regularly and add value to the group
- Frequent and regularly scheduled meetings allow members to know each other well
- Provides some networking tips at every meeting
- Members are expected to keep referrals within their group
- Potential to "cross-club" in larger organizations
- Regular referrals!

Cons:

- Some less-than-ideal referrals could feel forced and given to look good
- If the group size is small, you could spend as much time marketing for your referral group as your primary business.
- If the group size is too large, it could take longer to build relationships and give/get referrals.
- The membership fees, potential fines, and meals at meeting locations can get costly if you aren't receiving business from them.

- Growth can become more challenging if members are not networking outside of
- their referral group.
- It can get stale if no new members attend the meetings, and it's the same ten people every week.

Best practices:

- Attend different meetings before making a decision.
- Observe the size and culture of the group. How many referrals are passed at each meeting? Is everyone friendly? How's the energy level? Is the group growing?
- Take advantage of visiting other chapters where your industry is not represented.
- Volunteer for leadership positions.
- Be prepared to serve and give rather than be served and receive.
- Be intentional in meeting other members one-to-one to build relationships and trust, and learn about their business.
- Look at it as a long-term investment rather than a quick fix.

Organizations and Associations

Virtually all organizations and associations host networking events or meetings with networking opportunities.

Pros:

- All members typically share at least one thing in common
- Usually serve a greater purpose
- Meeting an extensive group of existing members
- Stay on top of industry trends
- Opportunity to position yourself in a complimentary industry or field

Cons:

- Less variety in the industries represented
- Events can have more programming than networking time
- Other participants will oftentimes be competitors
- Less frequent meetings can make relationship-building more challenging

Best Practices:

- Volunteer for leadership roles
- Become a valued part of the organization and get to know the other volunteers and leaders
- Join an organization or association where you are a complimentary fit
- Become an ambassador for the group and help with outreach to increase your exposure to the community

Resources to find in-person networking opportunities:

www.meetup.com provides opportunities to meet new people based on your interests. Whether you like jogging, workouts in the park, reading books, cooking, having philosophical discussions, or taking a cruise in your convertible on a sunny summer day, there's a group for you. Of course, you can also find business networking groups as well!

www.eventbrite.com will help you find meetings, events, workshops, seminars, and industry gatherings year-round!

www.myle.com is an up-and-coming events platform to help Make Your Life Entertaining. There are several social and business events to grow your network.

Your local Chamber of Commerce or Board of Trade will give you access to other local businesses and community events.

Local trade associations can be found on an internet search and will provide you with groups you can connect with.

Look into civic organizations like Rotary Club™, Kiwanis™, Lions Clubs International™, etc.

You can join a variety of networking and referral groups like CONNECTED Networking Group™, BNI (Business Networking International)™, AmSpirit™, Goldstar™, LeTip™, Synergy™, H7™, G7™, Network After Work™, and many more

Remember that there are also many "informal" networking opportunities at your church, kid's schools and activities, holiday gatherings, gym, etc. Search their calendars for upcoming events and jump in!

Chapter 23

Online Networking

Online networking has expanded the opportunities to meet new people worldwide from the convenience of your home or office. While the technology has been around for over a decade, it quickly gained wide acceptance at the beginning of 2020, when the global pandemic affected our lives forever.

As you serve and grow your relationships, new opportunities will present themselves in ways you never expected. You can create results through virtual events and online networking with the right mindset and strategy.

Never in the history of mankind have we had the convenience of instant access to one another! In addition to seeing each other on the screen, we can share our presentations, images, and documents and work on projects in real time!

Video chats are a great way to save time! In 1999, when I started my direct-sales business in Southern California, there was no option for a video chat. I was still working my retail job and trying to sneak in a sales appointment over lunch. If you've ever driven in the Los Angeles area, you know that lunch hour goes by fast when it includes driving anywhere due to the heavy traffic at all times. Nowadays, I could fit 2 to 4 appointments in that same amount of time!

When I started building my network in Ohio, I would drive all over town for my meetings. Even though there was no traffic in Columbus, Ohio (especially when compared to Los Angeles), it still took an average of 20 to 30 minutes of travel time between appointments.

So, for me to meet four people, that would be an hour-long meeting plus an hour of travel time for each. These 4 meetings would take up my whole day! Fast forward to today, and with the help of technology, we can have these virtual face-to-face chats without any travel time. This frees up an extra two to three hours per day! That's 10 to 15 extra weekly hours to reinvest in work, family, and self!

Over the past few years, people have become accustomed to video chat technology. It has become part of our new normal. Adopting a strategy to grow your network online and in person will help you achieve your results faster than ever.

To maximize your effectiveness in using online networking, I will share some tips and best practices with you.

> ADOPTING A STRATEGY TO GROW YOUR NETWORK ONLINE AND IN PERSON WILL HELP YOU ACHIEVE YOUR RESULTS FASTER THAN EVER.

Your goal for a virtual event is to be visible, add value, and make new connections. It's not much different than an in-person event, but the way you do it may be new to you, so I will outline the process below.

The first thing we will cover is the online networking event. Most organizations will host these on Zoom™, WebEx™, Microsoft Teams™, Remo™, or other virtual platforms.

The flow is similar to an in-person event with a host or moderator following an agenda. Ideally, online events will provide opportunities for audience participation and conversations in breakout rooms.

For online events, most of the conversations happen in the chat box while the speaker does their presentation.

I encourage you to actively listen and engage in the chat by responding to the speaker and conversing with fellow participants.

Every time you comment in the chat, your name appears in front of all attendees, and more opportunities become available to connect with other participants in a private chat.

The speakers love engagement from the chat since they don't receive the same type of feedback as they would when speaking to a live audience. This turns the chat into the one area where they can feel the energy and engagement of the audience.

Here are a few ideas on how you can positively impact any event through your chat comments.

Respond to any questions that they ask from the stage. If they ask, "Where are you joining from?" share that information. It can look something like this, "Hello, everyone. Chris here from Columbus, Ohio!"

As others share where they are joining from, feel free to engage with the speaker and other participants.

What you are doing here is making yourself visible. Whenever possible, you also want to have your camera on so that they can see you paying attention and being an active part of the event.

Nothing is more demoralizing for a virtual speaker than speaking to a screen full of blank squares with a person's name across the center. It provides them with no energy or feedback. From a speaker's viewpoint, it would be similar to speaking in front of a large audience where everyone was just looking down at their phone.

Turn your camera on, pay attention, be active, and be seen!

That is part of objective number one. Let's talk about objective number two, adding value.

Notice how being visible in a virtual event is not just self-serving. When I say to be visible, it doesn't mean it's all about "Look at me! Look at me!" Your being visible is also part of adding value to this virtual event.

You are creating more energy for the speaker. You are creating more engagement with other participants.

You are sharing answers in the chat and asking good questions that could benefit everyone at the event.

The third objective is to make new connections. People often wonder how they can do that when everyone is virtual. Remember the importance of mindset. Have the heart to serve and be there for others.

Every participant is looking to gain something from this event. Consider why they are attending. What are they interested in? They may be looking for additional knowledge. They may be interested in engaging with their peers. Or they may be interested in making new connections like you are.

Here's how you make new connections at a virtual event. If they have breakout rooms and you are in a smaller group, you can easily ask them if they want to stay in touch and share their contact information in the chat. This also allows you to share your information with them, where it is welcomed and not looked at as if you are spamming the public chat.

A quick tip here is to have your contact information saved on a note or document on your computer, making it easy to copy and paste into the chat. This will be helpful for all of the events that you join.

You will need to make new connections differently if there is no breakout group. Remember how you've been adding value and having conversations with the speaker and other participants in the chat? If there is someone you want to meet, send them a private message.

In the private chat message, you could say something like, "Hi Cyndy! Good seeing you here! I would love to stay in touch. What's the best way to stay connected?" They can send you their contact information and vice versa.

This is just an example, so feel free to modify it to fit your style and personality and make it relevant to your conversations. Being engaged in the chat opens up these doors for connections and relationships.

Remember, your goals for virtual events are the same as those at an in-person event. Be visible, add value, and make new connections.

Now that you are familiar with networking online at events, let's talk about networking online in small groups and one-to-one meetings. With smaller groups and one-to-one meetings, it's common practice for everyone to have their cameras on.

Test your system in advance to ensure that your camera, microphone, and speakers are working correctly. You also want to have good lighting and a distraction-free background.

With the growth in popularity of virtual meetings, it has become more casual than formal. So the occasional barking dog, kids needing attention, delivery men knocking on the front door, etc., are offered much more grace nowadays. I share this, so you don't worry about everything being perfect. Most people extend much more grace because many experience the same challenges working from home.

Best practices for small group and one-to-one networking meetings are similar to what you would do at a face-to-face meeting. Allow the other person to speak and share. If you are in a group, take responsibility and ownership to allow everyone equal speaking time unless someone has already assumed that role.

Setting clear objectives up front is helpful to everyone in maximizing their time. This includes the topic or topics, the objective of your time together, and even the anticipated time frame for your meeting.

As you wrap up your conversation, clearly identify the next step for everyone involved. Once your event is completed, whether big or small, you will follow the same practice of updating your notes.

Online networking is a very efficient and effective option nowadays with all the available tools. Become familiar with them and enjoy the new connections!

Chapter 24

How Do I Prepare for My First In-Person Event?

The thought of attending your very first in-person event can be downright frightening. Many common fears revolve around not knowing what to do and how things work.

I will share how to prepare for your first event in this chapter by providing tips and answering some common questions. Even if you are a seasoned networker, you will still find some great tips and best practices to make your networking more fun and effective.

Here's the first common question. What should I wear? Do your research to get insights into the organization and the event so that you can plan your attire. You can look online for photos or videos of prior events to give you a better idea of proper attire.

If there is a contact person on the invitation, feel free to message them and ask what the dress code is if it is not already stated in the promotional materials. For most events, the dress code is "business casual." Business casual can mean a lot of things to a lot of people. I advise you to wear something comfortable that represents you, your business, and your brand.

If unsure, lean towards overdressing rather than under-dressing, especially with it being your first event. You can also bring a suit jacket or sports jacket and leave it in the car in the case when you show up, you dis-cover that your idea of "business casual" is different from theirs.

What should I bring? My advice here is to travel as lightly as possible. Try not to bring anything that will occupy your hands. It can make you look clumsy as you try to hold a beverage or a plate of hors d'oeuvres while attempting to exchange business cards.

If you bring a purse or a bag of some type, bring one that can be hung over your shoulder so that you aren't holding it all night. I also recommend not bringing your flyers or other handouts because this occupies your hands and the people you are handing them to. Instead, develop an online flier that is easy to share electronically with someone interested in that information.

Bring your business cards or your electronic business cards. I like having actual cards in addition to digital cards because, for many people who have a physical card, it's nice to be able to make an exchange. As discussed in prior chapters, it is something tangible and should be something you are proud of.

Another helpful tip is to bring breath mints. Gum is ok, but you must be careful not to let it be a distraction by chewing during conversations. Having breath mints will give you some assurance that you are not being offensive without knowing it. Since you will be doing a lot of talking, it also helps you not to get dry mouth.

Map the venue in advance. Make sure that there isn't more than one listing for a similar name, so you don't go to the wrong place. Double and triple-check the address.

Anticipate the time of day you will be traveling for any possible traffic or detours. I advise you to arrive 30 minutes early to allow extra time to accidentally take a wrong turn or find parking. Especially if you are meeting in a downtown area or a location with limited parking.

Being early will help reduce anxiety, you'll find a parking spot much easier, and it will allow you to meet the organizers and volunteers before everyone else arrives.

Introduce yourself to the volunteers and organizers whenever possible. They may be scrambling to get everything set for the event, so offer to help if there is anything you can do. Most of the time, they will say no, but the gesture is appreciated and remembered.

If the volunteers are already at the welcome desk ready to greet attendees, you can start conversing with them, learning more about the event flow, and building rapport with them before everyone arrives.

The fact that they are volunteering means they probably know more people, and because they are active in the organization, they will be great connections for you.

You are now ready for your first event! The next chapter will explore how to "work" this event.

Chapter 25

What Are the Best Practices for "Working an Event?"

Congratulations, you are now at your first event! In this chapter, I will walk you through every component needed to "work" this event like a pro!

If you are feeling some anxiety, don't worry, that's completely normal. Anxiety and excitement produce very similar physiological responses, such as an increased heart rate, sweaty palms, shallow breathing, nervousness, etc.

Shift your mindset. Instead of saying that you are anxious, say that you are excited about your first event! There has to be some truth to that, right?

After meeting with the organizer or volunteers and early arrivals, you have a better idea of the flow of the event. Most start with open networking, which we described in a previous chapter. This is free time where you can meet anyone and everyone in the room. The buzz and ambient noise in the room will continue to increase as more and more people engage in conversations.

Where should I stand?

Some people believe it doesn't matter where you stand at an event, but it does matter. Here is my reasoning for that. Where would you want to be positioned if you purchase a vendor booth for an event? Would you want to be in the back corner with very little traffic? Or would you want to be in the front, where everyone needs to pass by your booth? Of course, you would want to be in the front! So, if you have a choice of where to stand, stand where you will get the most visibility and opportunities to connect!

How should I stand?

Now that you are in the best area of the room, you need to be properly positioned to improve the connections you are about to make. One fear that is fairly common for new networkers is not wanting to interrupt an existing conversation. Makes sense. We don't want to be rude. But guess what? Other people are also worried about the same thing.

While conversing with someone, others will be hesitant to interrupt your conversation. Here's the solution. It's all in the way that you stand. If you and I are having a conversation and standing squared up, facing each other, making eye contact as we talk, the impression we give off is that this is a "closed circle."

This would be a great strategy if we didn't want to be interrupted. We would avoid eye contact with anyone who might interrupt our conversation.

So, to encourage more people to join and facilitate more connections, we do the opposite. Instead of standing directly across from each other, we use an open stance creating an "open circle." We accomplish this by standing in such a way that there is a space for a third person to join our conversation. This can be done with larger groups as well.

Most of your small group members will not be aware of this, so it's up to you to make room in your circle for another person or persons and make them feel welcome to join. It can be as simple as making brief eye contact, smiling, or waving at them to join you.

This technique subconsciously makes you more likable because you reduce others' anxieties while welcoming them into the conversation.

How do I start the conversation?

The nice thing about networking events is that you know that everyone is there to meet others. This makes it a different experience than trying to meet strangers in public!

At the beginning of my networking workshops, I often ask attendees about their greatest fears regarding networking. One of the most frequent fears is knowing how to start a conversation and what to say.

This should be reassuring for you, knowing that you are normal and, secondly, you are not alone! Many of the people you meet will have this same anxiety or fear. As you help to alleviate others' stress, yours will disappear, and more people will gravitate towards you.

The easiest way to start the conversation is to introduce yourself with your name and ask them for theirs. When they introduce themselves, actively listen to capture their name the first time. Once they are done with their introduction, repeat their name at least once or twice. For example:

Chris, "Hi. My name is Chris. Nice to meet you. What is your name?"

Cyndy, "Hi, Chris. Nice to meet you as well. My name is Cyndy."

Chris, "It's a pleasure meeting you, Cyndy! So, Cyndy, tell me a little more about you and what you do."

Feel free to utilize whatever language and style fit your personality and situation. The example above helps you see how easy it is to repeat their name naturally. If you often forget names, this tip should help you actively listen and remember their name.

If their name is the same as a good friend or a family member, that is another way to restate their name as a natural part of the conversation. If you meet somebody with an unusual or unique name, ask them to say it again. If you still don't completely understand their name, ask them," How do you spell that?" Repeat to your best ability to get the proper pronunciation while welcoming them to correct your pronunciation until you get it right.

How do I continue the conversation?

Immediately after sharing and exchanging your names, most people expect you to ask about what they do, so feel free to ask away.

Let's say they share with you that they are launching a new business selling home-grown honey. You could easily follow up with questions like, "How did you become interested in homegrown honey?" "What stage of development is the new business at?" "Where is your business located?" "What are your goals for expansion?" There are tons of additional questions that you could ask, but this is just a small example. Follow your natural curiosity and ask away!

Asking these follow-up questions shows a genuine interest in learning more about them. Your mindset here is that you really want to get to know them as a person and get to know about their business. In most cases, they will also ask great questions about you and your business.

Keeping the Home Field Advantage

There is some strategy involved here as well. In my workshops, I like to share a story called "The Home Field Advantage." The lesson in the story revolves around a baseball game and the home team's advantage. For one, they play in familiar territory and in front of their fans.

But the biggest advantage is the fact that the home team bats last. That is an advantage because if they have the lead, they don't need to bat! They've already won the game. If they are behind in the ninth and final inning, they get another chance to bat. The advantage of batting second is they know what they need to accomplish.

For example, if they are down by one run, they may utilize a different strategy than if they are down by three runs.

So how does this relate to networking? By speaking second, you have an advantage. The advantage is that you have learned about the other person, which means you can tailor your Modular Introduction to be relevant to them. Remember that you have several variations of your Modular Introduction that you can adjust to fit your audience.

This gives you a distinct advantage over someone with a single canned elevator speech that they use for all situations.

Many people are so interested in sharing their introduction that they don't have the capacity to listen. Their brain is occupied with what they are about to say. This means that if you do your introduction first, there's a good chance that they will not be listening.

If they ask you to introduce yourself first, don't worry. Simply give your short modular introduction, then turn it around and ask them what they do. You'll maintain the home-field advantage without "insisting" that they answer first.

After a natural conversation, they will likely ask you for more details about what you do. You can share your Modular Introduction in a manner that is interesting and relevant to them because you've tailored it to fit your audience!

Take a step back and look at the favorable conditions you've created.

First, you started the conversation by making it more comfortable for them. You started with just your name without sharing what you do yet. You invited them to share a little bit more about what they do, and you asked follow-up questions to understand better who they are and their goals.

Since they had already shared about themselves, they had a greater capacity to listen and understand when they asked about you and what you do. Because you have several variations of your introduction available, you can share the one that will be the most relevant to your new connection. Your new relationship is off to a great start!

After you've each shared your professional introductions, it's time to deepen the relationship. You don't need a long time to build a strong connection. You just need to learn a few of these skills.

People are attracted to others who are like themselves. By identifying commonalities, your new relationship can be strengthened very quickly. Here are some ideas to help you get to the good stuff.

You can ask, "What are your favorite activities when you aren't working?"

"Do you have any upcoming travel plans?"

> PEOPLE ARE ATTRACTED TO OTHERS WHO ARE LIKE THEMSELVES. BY IDENTIFYING COMMONALITIES, YOUR NEW RELATIONSHIP CAN BE STRENGTHENED VERY QUICKLY.

"Outside of work, what are some things you're looking forward to over the next few months?"

"Where did you grow up?"

"What brought you here?"

"What are your favorite hobbies?"

"What's your favorite restaurant?"

"Did you play any sports growing up?"

You get the idea. You are trying to open the conversation to anything not work related that helps you get to know them as a person and anything that gets you closer to commonalities.

Do not ask ALL of these questions. Select one and go from there. Ask a question that you are sincerely interested in knowing the answer to, and ask questions that would not cause an awkward reply.

How do I keep the conversation from getting awkward?

Examples of questions that might have an awkward reply are, "Are you married?" This may put them in an uncomfortable spot if they are going through a divorce, or maybe they haven't found their soulmate yet and might feel bad about being alone.

Another bad question is, "Do you have any kids?" You might run across somebody that can't have kids but wants to. Or they might be in the middle of a custody battle, and it causes some anxiety.

Ask open-ended questions that allow them to share something about themselves that will lead to positive and fun connection opportunities.

Many new networkers worry about what they are going to say. Focusing on the other person eliminates that fear because you are just having a conversation. Having a conversation is much more natural than delivering a memorized pitch.

What about small talk?

Common small talk topics are the weather, sports, and current events. These are great places to start but not good places to stay for any extended period of time. Here's a quick tip. Avoid sensitive and potentially divisive topics like politics and religion. If it starts going down that path, change the topic quickly!

Your new skills will create more meaningful conversations and help prevent the awkwardness of someone going into full presentation mode, becoming salesly, or the conversation getting stuck in small talk mode.

How do I wrap up the conversation?

When you're at a networking event, you want to limit your conversations so that you can meet more than just one person. I would say to go by feeling and trust your intuition on how long you should be talking to somebody.

I don't believe we should be flying around the room handing out your business card every two to three minutes after making your pitch. But I also don't believe you should be talking to the same person for the entire event.

Once you've completed your introductions and learned a little about each other beyond your professions, it's time to wrap up this conversation so you can each have a new conversation with somebody else.

A good way to wrap up is by saying, "I enjoyed meeting you! I'd love to continue the conversation. What's the best way for us to stay in touch?" At this point, exchange contact information which you know how to do from the Business Card and Contact Management chapter.

Be the connector.

Even if this is your first event, and you didn't know anyone before attending, you can be the connector. Here's how it works: You're at the event and just met Ronnie. You had a great conversation and wrapped up your conversation with Ronnie.

Now, you and Ronnie float around the room until you find somebody else new to meet. Remember what I shared earlier in this chapter about creating open circles? If you met Cyndy when you first arrived and you have just met Ronnie, why not invite Cyndy into your open circle and introduce Cyndy to Ronnie?

You can even share a little about what you learned about them with each other and why it would be beneficial for them to meet each other. As they start their conversation, it frees you up to engage with a new person you haven't met yet.

All this happens while you are in a visible area of the room as others see you introducing people to one another. You will become the center of influence, attracting more people to want to talk to you. Not bad for a first event, right?

Step 5
Develop Strong Relationships

Chapter 26

What It Means to Have a "Strong Relationship"

How do you measure the strength of your relationships? We live in a world of social media. It's not unusual for someone to have thousands, hundreds of thousands, or millions of followers. While those numbers may look impressive, the accurate measure of the strength of your relationships is in the responsiveness, access, and reciprocal value exchange.

When I was chasing numbers on social media, Instagram to be exact, my goal was to reach 10,000 followers. After reaching 10,000 followers, Instagram would unlock some additional perks and features. I followed the program for about six months but didn't reach 10,000 followers.

I did reach 5,000 followers, however. While getting all of these followers in a short time was exciting, my news feed had changed. I no longer saw posts made by my friends because my newsfeed was filled with all of these new strangers' posts. They were now following me, and I was following them, but there was no connection. I didn't know them, nor did they know me. If I private messaged them or they private messaged me, there was a good chance that we would have ignored each other's messages.

This shows that the numbers have nothing to do with the strength of your relationships. If we've never met, but you are reading this book, we have a relationship because of this connection. Let's take it a step further, though. Let's say you sent me an email requesting to meet, and we scheduled a 15-minute call to get to know one another better. Our relationship just became stronger. The more that we share in common and the more that we interact with each other, the stronger our relationship becomes.

Think about the person that you trust the most in this entire world. Who is the person that you would go to if you were to receive some bad news? Who is the person that you knew would stand up for you if someone was treating you unfairly or bullying you? Who is the person that would stay up with you until 2 a.m. to help you through a crisis? Who is the person that you knew would be the first to raise their hand to help you move? If you were to rate the strength of this relationship on a scale of one to ten, what number would you give this person? I consider them a ten!

Most people you run across will not be close to a ten. You will have very few tens in your life. If you had one ten, you could consider yourself blessed.

When you meet somebody new, they would be a one. They could be a two or a three if they were incredible people. But in most cases, somebody new is a one. Just because somebody starts as a one doesn't mean they stay as a one. The strength of your relationship can go up very quickly!

For example, a person you just met at a networking event, someone sitting next to you in the waiting room at your doctor's office, or someone you met at church. They all start off as a one.

You follow the steps from previous chapters to build the relationship and get to know them over a 30-minute conversation. You discovered that you both went through a nasty divorce and bankruptcy and are in this new town starting your own businesses.

Your conversations were very transparent, uplifting, and encouraging. If they reached out to you with a request for help, how likely would you be to want to help? If you reached out to them with a request for help, how willing would they be to provide that help?

I think you'll realize the strength of your relationship is no longer one. You've only known this person for 30 minutes, but you feel connected! Has something like this ever happened to you?

The point I'm making here is that building strong relationships can take a long time to develop. However, with the right skills, finding common interests, and sharing relatable experiences, your relationship strength can quickly shoot straight up from 1 to an eight!

Let's transfer this idea into your networking efforts. Can you see how the skills you learned in the prior chapters can help you build relationships fairly quickly? You can do this even as a brand-new networker because networking isn't about how long you've been doing it. It's about creating genuine connections and authentic relationships with every person you meet.

As you build these relationships, it becomes easier to make an "ask." If you hesitate to ask, consider if you've invested enough into the relationship to make that request.

Search online for "wedding proposals." Inevitably you will find some videos that will touch your heart as the proposal is made and the proposal is accepted with tears of joy.

You will also find some videos of absolutely cringe-worthy proposals and rejections. The difference between the rejected proposal and the accepted proposal is determined by the strength of the relationship.

The person whose proposal was accepted most likely knew that the question would receive a resounding YES, 100%! The person whose proposal was rejected was probably nowhere near 100%.

The person who was rejected on the wedding proposal likely "over-asked" for the strength of their relationship. If they had asked to take a vacation together, a road trip, or a concert, the answer would more likely be yes.

Knowing your relationship's strength, you can make an appropriate ask. Let's apply this concept to the person we talked about earlier, who also went through a divorce and bankruptcy and started a new business just like you.

The things you shared in the initial conversation quickly took the strength of your relationship from a one to an eight! That's fantastic! But you are not in "marriage-proposal" territory yet. You cannot ask them for a big introduction to their CEO friend so you can make a business pitch. At least not yet. A more appropriate ask would be to meet them for coffee or lunch or request an introduction to other groups in which you share an interest.

Hope these examples provide you with a metric to determine the strength of your relationship and give you the confidence to make an appropriate ask that will likely result in a "Yes!"

Chapter 27

Building Real Relationships Through Social Media

If someone asked what social media meant to you, what would your answer be? For some, they would say that they love it! It's fun, and they stay in touch with their friends. Others would say it's a waste of time or it's filled with negativity.

Before we get deep into this chapter, take a minute and examine your answer to the question above. What does social media mean to you?

The reason why that's important is that the way you feel about social media will affect your actions, which will impact your results. In this chapter, I broadly use the term "social media" to include whichever platform you choose as your major, your minor, and your electives.

If you have had an overall view that social media is more of a waste of time and that it's mostly filled with negativity, you likely find that you don't use it very much or don't use it at all.

I started on social media in 2008 when Facebook was quickly gaining popularity. Up until this point, I hadn't used any social media. I didn't see why there was such a big appeal. As a very private person, it seemed odd that people would message each other publicly so everyone could see their conversations.

In 2012, when I began my networking journey, my circle of Facebook friends slowly grew outside of my immediate friends and family. When I met people at events, we would sometimes connect with each other on Facebook. I was still new to the whole networking thing, so this wasn't part of any strategy.

I found that we could get to know one another better by connecting on Facebook. Even though we had just met once, we felt we were staying in touch through our posts and comments.

Several years later, I realized that had we not connected shortly after meeting, neither of us would likely have remembered that we had even met!

Later that year, when I started intentionally using LinkedIn, I realized that the relationship could be built in both directions. We can strengthen that relationship by staying connected on social media with someone we met in person.

For someone we originally connected with on social media, we can strengthen the relationship by engaging with them on their posts and setting a time to meet over the phone, through video chat, or in person.

Most people start networking when they already have a need. They may need a job, or they may need to meet more prospects for their business. Perhaps they need financing for a project, or they may need to hit a sales quota. The problem is that they are not positioning themselves for long-term success. In reality, they are not even setting themselves up for short-term success!

Building relationships through social media is much easier than most people think. Those who believe it's challenging to build relationships on social media probably have an ulterior motive, an agenda, or a pitch, as the real purpose for connecting in the first place.

Let me ask you a question. Has somebody ever reached out to you on social media to pitch you something?

Maybe they started with a direct message saying, "Hello." And you already know it's got to be a pitch! Or perhaps they started complimenting you left and right, raising your suspicion because you had never talked to them. Or maybe they start asking you questions that feel like they are completing your "needs analysis" form!

The bottom line is that you can tell when someone has an agenda or is being disingenuous. You can tell right away, can't you? So if you can sense it coming from a mile away, don't you feel that others would have this same intuition if you were the one doing the pitching?

Building relationships on social media must come from a place of authenticity for it to work. Even though you communicate through a digital platform, your words communicate with a real person. Social media is simply a vehicle or a tool. Can you see how your mindset will impact your activity?

> BUILDING RELATIONSHIPS ON SOCIAL MEDIA MUST COME FROM A PLACE OF AUTHENTICITY FOR IT TO WORK.

When I look at my social media friends, connections, and followers, I see the names and the person their profile represents. Someone who has goals, family, challenges, doubts, and aspirations, just like you and I do.

Building relationships is about finding our common ground. And social media is an excellent tool for that. Think about it. You can now go on your social media feed and quickly discover what's important to someone. You can see how they spend their time outside of work. You can see their hobbies, favorite foods, recent travel adventures, and things like receiving an award, celebrating a birthday, an anniversary, or graduation!

You can quickly build relationships with many people by engaging with them on their posts. It would take forever to talk to 100 people individually. But by engaging in their posts, you can stay in touch with thousands of people through social media!

Here are some rules for engagement.

Be genuine. Put some thought into your comments. Make it encouraging and uplifting. Use it to start a dialog whenever possible. Remember that you are talking to a real person even though you are using a digital vehicle.

Most social media platforms don't show you all of your connections or friends' activities. They have an algorithm that determines what you see on your newsfeed based on your engagement. The more you engage intentionally with those you want to stay in touch with, the more you will see their activities, and the more they will see yours. So, if you don't see their activity on your account, don't be discouraged. It's not that people don't like you. They probably just aren't seeing it on their newsfeed.

Building relationships on social media requires you to be intentional. You will need to intentionally search for people that you want to connect with, see their activities, and engage with them there.

You will likely start to see each other in your newsfeed more often, which helps you to stay top of mind. After some engagement on their public posts, a direct message will be much more appropriate and better received. Too often, people "slide" into their DM's (direct messages) and look like spammers and scammers.

Treat your online interactions in a similar way that you would your in-person interactions. Start the dialog, find common ground, build trust, add value, then position yourself to make an ask. When you do, their response will most likely be, "Yes, I'd be happy to help!"

You can use social media to stay in touch with people you meet in person. You can use social media to meet new people whom you can develop relationships with and eventually meet in person! You can use social media to stay top of mind. You can use it to build trust. You can use it to showcase your expertise. You can use it to increase your influence!

The bottom line is to use it as a tool! View social media as a way for you to access people on demand. Not only can you reach people, but you can maintain connections with literally thousands of people in a short amount of time.

Be a light in the darkness. Share positivity and encouragement. Show love, care, and compassion regularly, and watch relationships grow and your influence increase.

Chapter 28

Mastering One-To-One Coffees, Lunches, and Calls

When I first started networking, I had no clue what to do at an event and was even more clueless as to what to do after the event. About a month after starting my journey, someone invited me to meet for coffee. I had never been asked to meet for coffee before, so I thought this was what I was supposed to be doing. So, I said, "Sure!"

I went to the coffee meeting about a week and a half later, armed with my sales brochures and laptop, ready to give a presentation if the opportunity presented itself. Remember, I had no clue how this was supposed to go down.

At the coffee meeting, I never shared anything about my business, even though that's what I thought the entire time. Instead, I was lucky enough to watch their sales presentation and about 40 or 50 slides for about an hour. I wasn't interested in buying anything but wanted to be polite, so I sat through the whole thing.

Since this was my first exposure to the coffee meeting, I thought this was how it was done. You set a coffee meeting, and you share your products. I started scheduling coffee meetings. I thought maybe it was just nicer terminology for "sales presentation." I did this for months.

Then I realized that I wasn't genuinely building stronger relationships. I was just doing more sales presentations. I felt in my heart that I wasn't doing this correctly.

I saw a slight increase in sales simply from the greater number of people I was meeting with, but it wasn't enough to justify the time and effort.

I realized I didn't go to my first coffee meeting to be pitched or buy anything. In the same way, when others met with me for coffee, they weren't there to be pitched by me or to buy anything from me.

How can this activity be productive if I don't want to buy from them, and they don't want to buy from me? I knew I was missing something.

Since I wasn't getting results from this activity, I changed my mindset. I started focusing outward instead of inward. I started considering what their wants and needs were rather than my own wants and needs. As soon as I did this, everything shifted.

For one, I experienced significantly lower anxiety because I was no longer worried about guiding the conversation to my sales pitch. It allowed me to be present and listen at a deeper level.

It allowed me to connect genuinely with the person instead of being intimidated by their role, title, or position.

Here are some tips for a productive one-to-one coffee meeting. First, select a place that is convenient for all parties.

The ideal meeting place has enough ambient noise to where you can speak in relative privacy without raising your voice. Meeting at a place that is too quiet can be awkward because everyone can hear your conversation.

Send a confirmation text or email to ensure nothing has changed, so you don't waste time driving across town for a no-show.

Arrive at least five minutes early to give you time to find a suitable place to sit and settle in. If you will be late, let the other person know as soon as possible and no later than your scheduled time.

Offer to buy the coffee. It could be the best investment of a few dollars you have ever made.

If you have an appointment immediately following your meeting time, it's a good practice to say so upfront, then you both have the correct expectation for how long you will be meeting. It will also avoid some awkwardness if they are in the middle of a story, and you say you must go. This would come across as you not being interested in their story.

Make sure you agree on the reason for your meeting. No one likes to be blindsided. You can be meeting to get to know one another better, you can be meeting to figure out ways to support and help one another, get some feedback, share an idea, or pitch your services! It's all good as long as you are in agreement.

If the person has something you immediately want or need, i.e., knowledge, connections, consultation, guidance, let them know up front that that is what you are looking for, and be willing to hire them or offer something in their favor.

Do not ever set a meeting of any type to "pick their brain." Remember to offer value first and determine the strength of your relationship before making an appropriate ask.

As an alternative, find ways to collaborate and reciprocate value. The next chapter will go deeper into how to add value to others.

> DO NOT EVER SET A MEETING OF ANY TYPE TO "PICK THEIR BRAIN." REMEMBER TO OFFER VALUE FIRST AND DETERMINE THE STRENGTH OF YOUR RELATIONSHIP BEFORE MAKING AN APPROPRIATE ASK.

Here are some best practices for lunch meetings. If possible, schedule your lunch meeting before or after the lunch rush. Starting your meeting at 11:30 or 11:45 can make a big difference in your wait time compared with starting your meeting at noon. If that time doesn't work for you, consider any time after 1:00 p.m. when most of the rush has passed.

Select a place that all parties agree on. This encompasses location, cuisine, and price.

Make sure the service time is fast enough to fit your time frame. If you only have an hour, you might not want to meet at a place with slow service.

If this is an essential meeting for you, pay for the lunch! If it's a mutual "get to know you" meeting, generally, each person pays for their own lunch.

If possible, select a seat away from heavy traffic areas like the front door or the kitchen. Make sure you leave a suitable tip.

Your one-to-one meetings are one of the most important steps in building quality relationships. It is also one step most people skip because it involves investing time and money.

Your one-to-one calls can be done on the phone or via a video conference platform. These follow the same guidelines as your coffee meeting. Some advantages are that they are more efficient since you don't have to travel, and it is easier to schedule shorter meetings when it's done over the phone or via video conference.

Make sure you are in a quiet place to take your call, preferably with a good internet signal or cell reception. If you are going to be in the car or on the road for your appointment, make sure you pull over for your call. The number one reason for this is safety, but it is more professional for them to have your undivided attention. By being parked, you also have the ability to take notes during your call.

To highlight the importance of one-to-ones, imagine two networkers starting their networking journey simultaneously. Both attend meetings, take notes, and connect on social media. But only one of them intentionally and consistently meets his or her connections for one-to-one phone, video, or lunch meetings. You will see a significant difference in the short and long-term results!

One-to-one meetings are where deep connections are made. They solidify the relationship and separate you from the 95% of the people who do not do this.

Stronger relationships lead to the potential for bigger asks and more opportunities!

Are you up for a challenge? Schedule at least one of each type of meeting (coffee, lunch, phone/video) with someone you already know to "catch up" or reconnect. You'll see how fun and effective these one-to-one meetings are! Next, schedule one of each type of meeting with someone you want to know better.

Track your results and enjoy the strengthened relationships and new friendships!

Chapter 29

Serving and Adding Value

In my early days of networking, I understood the concept of "adding value." The problem was that the only value I thought I had was the product I was selling.

No matter what products, services, or goods you offer, the number of people who purchase it will be a very small percentage of the people you talk to.

Do you remember the chapter on river fishing? By only thinking of our needs and wants, we easily overlook the value we can provide to others already within our ability. If you think your offerings are your main source of value to the marketplace, you are mistaken.

In this chapter, I will share several ways to add value that have nothing to do with the products, services, or goods; you offer.

You can add value with your knowledge. What seems like common sense to you may be a big revelation for somebody else.

You can add value with your skills. You may know how to write and can help with blogs, emails, and copyright items. You may know how to fix cars, and you can help prevent friends from getting overcharged.

You can add value with your connections. As we examined in prior chapters, networking is about being interconnected with one another. Remember the chapter on finding your black belt. Your introductions can open up a world of impact without even realizing it.

You can add value to your finances. You can invest your finances and help others with a vision, a dream, the know-how, and the opportunity that wouldn't happen without money.

You can add value with your creativity. In most cases, you either have creativity or you don't. If you have it, you can easily help others that don't. Your mind works in a way that makes it seem easy to come up with alternative solutions, create a unique design, or think outside the box.

You can add value with your listening skills. Sometimes people just need someone to listen. They may need someone to listen to a new idea as they flesh it out, or they may need someone to listen to some challenges they are experiencing, or they may need someone to listen while they vent. Remember that you are dealing with people, and everybody could use someone to listen.

You can add value with your support and encouragement. Your positive outlook and optimism can be a godsend for somebody experiencing doubts or fears about something they are encountering. By supporting and encouraging enough people, you can be sure that somebody will be there for you in your time of need.

As seen above, you can add value with any number of resources, and that is just a small sample. Notice that all of this value can be added and has absolutely nothing to do with the products, services, or goods you offer.

ADDING VALUE TO OTHERS DEEPENS YOUR RELATIONSHIP AND MAKES YOU MORE MEMORABLE, MEANING THAT YOU ARE MORE LIKELY TO STAY TOP OF MIND AND BE REFERRED WHEN THEY RUN ACROSS THE PERSON WHO COULD USE YOUR SERVICES.

Adding value to others deepens your relationship and makes you more memorable, meaning that you are more likely to stay top of mind and be referred when they run across the person who could use your services.

Here are some ways you can serve. If you are part of an organization, you can serve as a volunteer or as a leader. You do this as an actual act of service, not expecting anything in return. If you search online for "non-profit organizations," you could easily find ways to serve an organization where you are aligned with its mission.

Serving can take the form of a leadership role, it can take the form of a volunteer role, or it can take the role of helping anyone around you who is in need. This is not a transactional type of service. You are not keeping score. You are serving because you feel it is the right thing to do, and makes you feel good.

When you serve, you also get to meet like-minded individuals and groups who are service focused. Being in their presence will provide opportunities you could never have imagined.

Step 6
Build your Personal Brand and Community

Chapter 30

Build Your Personal Brand

Over the last decade, my personal brand has become "networking." Even though I started multiple businesses within ten years, I was still primarily known as the networking guru or the networking guy.

Even when I was not actively marketing my speaking services, coaching services, or courses, I would still get regular referrals from people I may have met years ago. This is what a personal brand can do for you.

In this section, we will explore ways to elevate you to start thinking much bigger. When most people start their networking journey, they primarily think of the goals they are trying to accomplish. That goal may be finding a new job, getting more supporters for their non-profit organization, generating leads, or increasing sales.

Those are all great goals. They can all be achieved much faster and more consistently by building your personal brand and creating a community around you. First, let's talk about your personal brand.

Your personal brand is much more than your logo, business cards, or website. You may not have thought of yourself as having a personal brand.

When choosing between you and someone else for your products, services, or goods, it's well-known that you need to differentiate yourself. Most try to do this with the number of years they've been in business.

Differentiating yourself can best be done by having a personal brand. If I was to ask you who you would recommend for my car that isn't running right, looking for a new home, or the restaurant that serves the most authentic street tacos, chances are you have a name at the top of your head of someone who could help. That person had developed a strong personal brand.

You may have also developed a strong personal brand yourself without realizing it. This personal brand may not even be related to your profession or field. But it's a personal brand nonetheless.

Think of a topic, subject, category, or interest that people often come to you for your advice or opinion. This could include financial advice, relationship advice, things to do on date night, or gardening tips!

If you have already built a personal brand that isn't your primary profession, there are ways that you can weave it in to differentiate yourself on your professional brand.

Let's say you are a great gardener with a green thumb and are starting your business in financial planning. You can easily integrate your love for gardening with your business. You can draw parallels between the process of having a healthy garden and having a healthy future.

Your framework can include preparing the soil, planting seeds, and protecting and nourishing those seeds until they grow abundantly. Each step can equate to building a healthy financial future for your clients.

Preparing the soil may be equivalent to a "needs analysis." Planting seeds may be a variety of investments. Protecting and nourishing those seeds may be the equivalent of keeping a close eye on market conditions and trends.

I have a friend who was a college football star and also played in the NFL. When he recently started in the insurance industry, his slogan was, "If your agent isn't 6'6" and 330 pounds, you are under-protected." He utilized his personal brand as a football player in his profession.

Think of what your personal brand may already be. Is it a hobby you have, like collecting classic cars, climbing mountains, cycling, martial arts, craft, or something else? Consider ways that you can integrate your personal brand into your profession.

Now you may wonder, "What do I do if I don't have a personal brand and don't know what I'm good at?" That's the position I was in when I first started my journey.

In the following chapters, we will explore some ways to develop your personal brand and, at the same time, build a community around you.

Chapter 31

What It Means to Have "Community"

When I first started networking in 2012, it was difficult for me to get a sales appointment. Fast forward to today, and I have the opposite issue, where I have to be intentional with my time to serve the people reaching out to me.

In 2012 I contacted people as an individual who needed to make appointments and get sales. Today I am no longer prospecting as an individual. I have established a large community of people I have served over the years that now refer me to potential clients.

Most people in the business world looking to accomplish a goal approach it as a "numbers game." While there is truth to additional sales and results from reaching out to many people, having a community can get you those same results with less effort and in less time.

In 2012, when I was "networking" to generate leads and prospects, the results were disappointing. Some of you may have tried networking and experienced some disappointment.

For most people, "networking" didn't work because they weren't really networking. They were "prospecting" at a networking event. There is a big difference between the two, even though they may look similar.

> FOR MOST PEOPLE, "NETWORKING" DIDN'T WORK BECAUSE THEY WEREN'T REALLY NETWORKING. THEY WERE "PROSPECTING" AT A NETWORKING EVENT.

I started my journey prospecting rather than networking. My sales increased simply because of the increased number of people I spoke to. If this were a baseball game, I would get more hits due to the added at-bats, but I would also have a lower batting average.

A sign that I was prospecting rather than networking was that I wasn't getting responses to my voicemails and emails. Or, in today's terms, I was being ghosted.

Has this ever happened to you? You send an email and get no response. You leave a voicemail and get no response. You follow up two or three more times, and still no response. At this point, you are wondering if you are bothering them or if they are just busy.

Should you keep on following up? Should you give up? If they weren't interested in what you were offering, you would appreciate a response telling you they were not interested instead of ghosting you. This is what happens when you are prospecting rather than networking.

Imagine attending an event and seeing that person who just ghosted you three or five, or ten times. Are they more likely to run up and hug you or pretend they didn't see you?

Not only does this prospecting approach lead to minimal results for the amount of work put in, but it also gets in the way of genuine connection. True networking will create strong connections, genuine friendships, and a community that is always there for you.

The prospectors can operate in this manner for years and still not have a community. Unfortunately, that's where most people get burned out in the process, then move on to a different company or even a different city because all of their leads have dried up.

A community is like being part of a large family, looking out for one another's interests. The relationships are genuine. You care about the people and not just if they would be a client.

Statistically, more people will never be your client compared to those who actually will. By overlooking building a community around you, you will continue chasing numbers until your leads have dried up.

Being part of a community goes well beyond your business or profession. It truly becomes like an extended family. By maintaining these relationships, you no longer get ghosted. You have dozens or even hundreds of people willing to support you any time you have a request. You also have people whom you can share life with.

Chapter 32

Embrace Diversity

We all tend to be attracted to others like us. It may be because we look similar, dress similarly, act similarly, and have common interests in movies, music, art, and hobbies. Maybe we grew up in the same neighborhood, have the same college major, or enjoy playing the same sports.

These commonalities help to create a natural bond between us. In an earlier chapter, we discussed how finding commonalities could be a great way to help us connect with one another.

When creating your community, too much similarity can be bad. While having a standard tie between your group is great, embracing diversity is essential.

Oftentimes diversity is thought of as having people of different nationalities and skin colors. While that is an accurate thought, diversity goes well beyond that.

Diversity also includes our perspectives on politics, religion, and other current affairs. Diversity includes our education, knowledge, skills, and talents. Diversity includes our demographic groups, socioeconomic status, and life experiences.

Hanging around people who think and act as you do can limit the synergy of the group. Consider a football team with 11 Tom Brady's on the field simultaneously. Tom Brady is arguably the best quarterback that has ever played the game. Having 11 Tom Brady's on the field would not likely be a winning combination. A winning football team is comprised of specialists who excel in their positions.

CREATING A DIVERSE COMMUNITY DOES NOT HAPPEN BY ACCIDENT. YOU MUST BE INTENTIONAL BECAUSE OUR NATURAL TENDENCY IS TO HANG AROUND PEOPLE LIKE OURSELVES.

In the same way, your network and community will have the winning formula when you include individuals who excel in each of their roles.

This is where true synergy occurs; the sum is greater than its parts. Creating a diverse community does not happen by accident. You must be intentional because our natural tendency is to hang around people like ourselves.

There is richness in being part of a diverse community. It will not only help you professionally, but it will also help you personally. You become much wiser and stronger when you hang around people with different likes, dislikes, and viewpoints. It gives you greater sensitivity to other perspectives that help you better relate to the world.

This subconsciously attracts even more diversity to your community.

We live in a world that quickly judges and criticizes others who are different. You get to be the glue that brings people together and helps bring more unity and peace to the world, starting with your small community.

Chapter 33

Finding Your Community

Some of you already have a community but haven't recognized or fully utilized it. Others are just starting to know that you do not yet have your community.

First, your community will likely be a mix of several communities, of which you become the center hub. As mentioned in a prior chapter, networking doesn't need to occur at a specific location or event. It can happen anywhere and everywhere you meet other people!

Here are some ways to find your community:

Identity groups you are already part of. Write them down. Once identified, you can go down your list and note your participation level within that group.

Take note of the people in that group you can serve and take note of the people that could help achieve your goals. Repeat this process for each of the groups you are already part of.

If you are not very active in participating in groups or organizations, you can find plenty of opportunities with an online search.

Resources that would be particularly helpful are Eventbrite™, Meetup™, MYLE™, Facebook™ Groups, LinkedIn™ Groups, and many more.

Also, search for organizations and associations that will put you in touch with the people you want in your community. You will want to participate in groups with people in a similar field and with similar goals to stay updated on industry trends and new developments.

Create a balance by joining organizations and associations where you are complementary to that industry.

For example, suppose you were a realtor. In that case, you could join your local realtor association meetings to learn of trends in the market and market conditions, best practices from other realtors, and gain credibility from being part of the group.

One of the downsides to this is that most of the other members are also your competitors. The strategy to help create more collaborative relationships is to join organizations and associations for a complementary field.

For example, if you were a realtor, you could join your local mortgage banker association and meet loan officers and bankers who would complement what you do.

Your local Chamber of Commerce is a great organization to get started with. There will be many existing connections in your local community that you can tap into as you build relationships with them.

You will find that certain groups or organizations are more of a direct benefit to your professional career. But don't overlook the social groups and clubs that can be helpful in an indirect way.

Once you go down this path, you will have more groups to participate in than you have the time for. You can then narrow down your focus and spend more time with those groups that will provide the most mutual benefit.

Chapter 34

Creating Your Community

Now that you've identified several different groups to meet people, it's time to create your own personal community. By joining the groups above, you become part of their community. You gain more visibility, credibility, and influence as you become more active in those groups.

In this chapter, I'll share the benefits and strategies to create your own community. The small gathering is one of the best ways to get started, even if you are brand new to this.

A small gathering can be as simple as inviting a handful of people to meet over coffee or lunch. The people you ask are intentionally chosen because you know that they would add value to one another and yourself.

Here is an example following the real estate professional in the previous chapter. Let's say that you are a real estate agent. Think of all the complementary roles involved in a real estate transaction. What would happen if you brought people from these different roles together? i.e., Mortgage Lender, Real Estate Attorney, Home Inspector, Appraisal Company, Handyman, Home Improvement, Title Company, Notary, etc.

They are all in complementary fields and not in direct competition with one another. They would likely be able to share referrals with one another once they've built trust.

The fact that you brought them all together positions you as the connector. As the connector, you become memorable and are more likely to stay top of mind with each of these people in complementary fields. This will lead to more referrals for you!

This small gathering can be held as frequently as once a week, once a month, or once a quarter. The more often you host these consistently, the greater your results will be.

You will notice that your gatherings will start to grow. These small gatherings don't need to be restricted to fields directly involved with your industry.

Remember that your community will be comprised of several fields and professions. You want to have a diverse community! Many of your best connections will come from your least-expected sources.

Growing your personal community is as much a part of your growth plan as your immediate sales goals. No matter what your personal or professional goals are, you will be able to accomplish them much faster and with much less effort with your community.

The small gathering is a significant first step. At each meeting, you can create an agenda that includes a brief business introduction and an activity to get to know each other personally. You can also have everyone share something they are looking for added support with or a specific referral they seek.

As your personal community grows, you can host large events where you can bring together all of your connections. This will position you as a leader and influencer in your city and possibly the world, depending upon where all of your connections reside.

Everyone wants to gain access to the "centers of influence." By creating your own personal community, you become the center of influence that others want to meet.

Building your own personal community happens while you are pursuing your short-term goals. It will pay dividends for years to come and create opportunities you never imagined possible.

Chapter 35

Your Brand, Your Community, and You

In the last chapter, you discovered the importance of building your personal brand and building your own personal community. These are essential components to growing your network and accomplishing your goals.

Even though this may all be new to you, you can do it!

I attended my first networking event in 2012 and started my own networking group in 2013. You can decide on your group's culture by creating your own community.

I wanted to create a group that made everyone feel welcome and like they were part of the family. This was important to me because, as a former shy introvert, I knew the anxiety of attending an event for the first time and not knowing anyone there.

In 2014 I started training others how to network properly because, like myself, most people were never taught how to network. Since then, hundreds of thousands of people have been impacted by this training.

My vision is to create connected communities worldwide because it will help individuals grow, help businesses thrive, and bring unity to a world that greatly needs it.

What happens when you build your personal brand and your personal community?

If you were an author, would you sell more books? Yes!

If you were a speaker, would you get more speaking gigs? Yes!

If you were a coach, would you get more clients? Yes!

If you were an entrepreneur, would you expand your business? Yes!

If you were in business development, would you increase your sales? Yes!

If you were a job seeker, would you get more offers? Yes!

If you were a nonprofit leader, would you get more donors and volunteers? Yes!

Think about the bigger purpose behind growing your personal community. In addition to accomplishing your own goals, imagine how many others you would be able to help accomplish theirs!

This leads us into the final step of this seven-step journey toward accomplishing your goals, your authentic relationships, and your connected communities.

In the next step, you will learn how to create winning collaborations and partnerships for accelerated and sustained growth.

Step 7
Create Winning Collaborations and Partnerships

Chapter 36

"Networking Up"

When you look back at my networking journey, you will see that I started by thinking small. I was just looking to meet more people that I could prospect to buy my services.

As you explore your journey, you probably also started or are starting by thinking small. Over the following few chapters, you will discover ways of thinking bigger.

Networking has opened many doors and possibilities over the last few years. It has transcended lead generation and has transformed into creating winning collaborations and partnerships.

These collaborations and partnerships increased my visibility, influence, and impact on the communities we collectively serve.

This book is intended for the first-time networker, but these lessons will serve even seasoned networkers because most are never taught these skills.

My original purpose for this book was to help the newer networkers to overcome their fears, gain confidence, and to see how this can help them achieve their goals. The next few chapters will help you to perform at a high level, even though you are newer to the networking arena.

Let me introduce the concept of "Networking Up."

Networking up is connecting with people in circles above yours.

When I was in direct sales, a big part of the business was recruiting more sales associates. What often happens is that the new associate would recruit people at their level or below.

If you thought of yourself as a "seven," you would feel comfortable talking to your peers who were also "sevens." You would also feel comfortable recruiting people who were "fives" or "sixes" because they looked up to you.

As time goes on, the strength of your team diminishes because you and everyone else on your team follow the same pattern of recruiting at their level or below.

Networking up would be the equivalent of recruiting "eights," "nines," and "tens" into your business. The eights, nines, and tens have more connections than you, more influence than you, and oftentimes more resources than you.

Those who understood this principle in direct sales became very successful.

WHEN WE TALK ABOUT NETWORKING UP, WE'RE TALKING ABOUT EXPANDING THE PEOPLE IN YOUR NETWORK TO INCLUDE THOSE WHO HAVE MORE CONNECTIONS THAN YOU, MORE INFLUENCE THAN YOU, AND MORE RESOURCES THAN YOU.

When we talk about networking up, we're talking about expanding the people in your network to include those who have more connections than you, more influence than you, and more resources than you.

Remember that networking is all about connections. Networking Up gives you more connections than if you were to network across or down. The good news is that you can Network Up quickly through your individual efforts or through your existing community.

To Network Up, you must be consistent in everything previously discussed in this book. Each step is what leads you to the following step. You'll notice that this is part of the seventh and final step, the one that produces the most significant rewards for your networking efforts.

Everything you've done to this point has positioned you to accomplish your goals and open up unlimited opportunities!

Think of a few people that you would classify under Networking Up. How can they support you in achieving your goals? What would be the benefit of having them in your network?

Some of you may not have considered this a pathway to your goals, even though it's the fastest way to achieve them. Some of you know exactly who you want to connect with but don't know how to make it happen.

Now that you understand the concept of Networking Up, let's explore ways to make this a reality.

Chapter 37

Identifying the Bigger Wins

It's challenging to accomplish big wins if you can't even visualize the big win. There are bigger wins available for you and those in your network.

We live in a whole new world. There has been more technological advancement in our lifetime than there has been in all of the existence of the world.

Our world is changing faster than ever. That means that an opportunity is created every time change occurs.

Let me share a personal example of identifying bigger wins. In March 2020, we were placed on lockdown due to the Coronavirus Pandemic. Our business at this point revolved around in-person gatherings.

When the lockdown was first announced, and everything around us had been forced to shut down, reality had set in. I never thought anything like this was even possible. But here we were.

For about a week straight, I went into panic mode, wondering how we would survive this lockdown and still generate revenue. But then I reminded myself that every change and every crisis creates opportunity.

In November of 2019, just a few months before the lockdown, we innovated how we connected people by adding a unique virtual platform to host events remotely for people who couldn't attend in person.

We shifted all our in-person events to a virtual replica of that event. This wasn't just another video chat; this was more of a simulated gathering happening in the virtual world.

We mastered creating connections utilizing technology. Many organizations at this time suffered greatly. Their members were unable to stay connected with one another. They lost momentum. And they lost revenue due to canceled events.

Following the steps outlined in this book and serving first, I opened up my schedule to help other organizations get through this difficult time. I shared tips, tools, and strategies we had been using to continue growing our group.

Word got around, and some of these organizational leaders eventually asked if I could run virtual events for them! They offered to pay me money to solve this problem for them, and Borja Virtual Conferences and Events was born!

Here's where identifying the bigger win comes in. Instead of looking at generating one-time clients, we focused on becoming an extension of their team, which resulted in us becoming their event partner for all of their events!

In the first two years, we helped our partners generate over $2,000,000 in revenue and donations while earning a fair amount for ourselves.

So what are the bigger wins you can identify for yourself and your network? What are some existing problems or challenges that you can solve?

How can you create a win for yourself and those you want to connect with in your Networking Up category? It could be something you can do directly, or you could create a win for them through someone else in your network.

Think long term, and think big. We now live in a world where the only constant is change. Change presents challenges, but it also provides opportunities!

Build your network, build your brand, increase your influence, and keep your eyes open for ways to serve others and create bigger wins.

Chapter 38

Gaining Access to More Exclusive Circles

One of the main challenges in "networking up" is gaining access. Successful people are typically busier and are very intentional about where their time goes.

They may not be out at public networking events very often. They prefer to network among their peers, such as other C-Suite executives and fellow influencers.

Here's an example of why this may be the case. I once invited a prestigious CEO in my network, who runs a global company and is a best-selling author, to one of our large networking events. We had built a rapport over time to where he could honestly share this response with me.

He said, "Chris, I love what you do in the community. And I appreciate what you do to bring people together. No offense to you, but I don't attend these events because I typically get nothing but pitches because of my position in the company. I'd love to support you, and if there is anything else I can do to be of service, don't hesitate to ask."

I was thankful for his candid reply. Remember the earlier chapter where we talked about getting ghosted? In this case, we had built a strong enough relationship for a straightforward, appreciative, and thoughtful reply. Signs of a solid relationship! But let's continue with the lesson.

Since the people you want to connect with may not be regular participants at your local networking events, you need to find alternative ways to access them.

To successfully access them, you need to be intentional and do your research. You must be very specific and have a well-thought-out plan.

Here are some strategies that will help you gain access to your nines and tens, as referenced in the chapter on Networking Up.

Here are some places where you can meet your nines and tens.

Organizations - There are many service organizations like Rotary International, Kiwanis, The Rotary Foundation, Lions Club International, and many more that you could find with a search of "service clubs and organizations."

These organizations have members who volunteer to serve and impact their local community. Many members are very well connected from current or prior leadership roles.

Some of these organizations have been declining in membership over the last two decades, which would create a unique opportunity for you to bring your enthusiasm and energy to the group.

Make sure you serve at that organization with the right heart, not "using" the organization to accomplish your goals. Serve to serve! Be a servant with everything in you, from your heart to your head and your hands to your feet.

Conferences and Summits - These are typically more significant events that happen quarterly or annually. Your ideal connection may be the event organizer, a sponsor, a speaker, or a participant.

This is a great way to have a chance encounter with them in the venue lobby and meet for the first time or a great way to connect face to face for a few brief moments and set up a phone call or set up a meeting with them.

Banquets and Awards ceremonies - These events often attract the highest caliber people. Remember the saying that birds of a feather flock together? That applies here as well.

Some events may be invitation-only, while others will have tickets available for purchase. Since these events are often formal attire, you will get to look and feel your best as you mix and mingle with high-caliber connections.

You will also meet many great connectors here who can introduce you to the specific people you want to meet.

Mastermind groups - This is one of the fastest and easiest ways to get into proximity with your ideal connection. A great connection is inherently made by being in the same mastermind group. This also positions you to meet more as "peers," which considerably levels the playing field.

Quality masterminds will have a strict application process and require an investment of $5,000 to $10,000 on the low end and $50,000 to $100,000 on the high end. But just joining isn't enough.

You need to be active and continue to serve your Mastermind group. If you do everything you've learned from this book and apply it to your Mastermind group, you are well on your way to success through high-level connections!

Here are some actions you can take to gain access to your Dream Team.

Visualize the person you want to connect with and see how you can provide value, become known, and build an authentic relationship. Repeat the process for each additional person.

Leave a review or testimonial - Most influencers and high achievers will have a way for you to leave a review for them. It may be a LinkedIn recommendation, Podcast review, Amazon book review, Google review, or a third-party site for you to leave a testimonial. You can leave a review on a talk they've done, a show they were on, a presentation they did, a book they've written, a service you've utilized, or simply how they have positively impacted your life. This will catch their attention very quickly.

It works well with the other steps and strategies you're learning in this chapter. As a side benefit, your name also shows up on their page in front of their audience, providing you with added visibility.

Promote them - Since you've done your research and know what is important to them, why not promote them and recognize them to show your appreciation? This can be done on any social media platform you utilize.

In most cases, this will be LinkedIn, but there may be other times when Facebook, TikTok, or Twitter may be the best platform for this.

Provide a meaningful introduction - You can introduce them to somebody who would be a good fit for them or may be interested in their products or services. Make an introduction that would be beneficial for them.

I prefer to use LinkedIn for these introductions over email because each person can see the other person's profile, so it isn't like a "blind date." Also include why you are making the introduction and how it will benefit both of them by their meeting.

Serve beside them - Remember those organizations we discussed earlier in this chapter? Don't just join them to be added to their membership directory. Become an active contributor.

There is something about serving alongside someone that creates an instant bond. Like everything we've covered in this book, this isn't about transactional serving. You are serving from the heart. The way in which you are serving will provide you with opportunities to create the authentic relationships that you are seeking to develop.

Here are some timely opportunities that open the door for you.

New book launch - If your ideal connection is launching a new book, they want to make as much impact as possible by getting it into more hands and increasing their sales to reach best-seller status. This is a great opportunity for you to pitch in and support by purchasing a book or multiple books, leaving an Amazon review (video review for bonus points), and officially joining their book launch team if they have one.

Attend the launch party if possible and make introductions to associations, schools, groups, and organizations that may be interested in ordering bulk quantities.

New course or program - You can enroll in their program and become their top student. Become a testimonial for their course by applying what you've learned and getting results. This is even more important to them than the money you paid to join the course. This will instantly put you on their radar and open up opportunities for a deeper connection.

New non-profit campaign - If you know of a non-profit organization they run or are supporters of, you can start by donating. In addition, you can share and promote on your social media platforms. Include some kind words and why you decided to support that organization. Compliment your ideal connection and tag them in the post. Do not make this about your donation. Your primary focus on this post should be on the benefit the non-profit is providing and how you discovered it through your ideal connection.

Their social media - If they are active, you can regularly engage in their posts to add your own insights, encouragement, support, and positivity. Every time you comment, your name and profile picture become visible to them and all their other followers.

If you are a little intimidated by engaging directly with their posts, don't worry about it. They created the post in the first place to get engagement. You can build real relationships through social media. Think of it as a group text message where you have direct access to them. Regularly engaging with their posts will create a favorable environment to send a direct message and begin a one-to-one dialog.

For all this to work, be comfortable and confident in your value and what you bring to the table. That's why this chapter is at the end of the book. You must be prepared for the moment and create opportunities with intention and perseverance. Remember that you aren't trying to connect with them so that you win and they lose. Connecting with them will create a win/win for both of you!

Focus on developing real relationships, which will take time. You increase your chances of success by thinking of a bigger win for them. Everyone has needs. Discover what those needs are and create a plan to fill those needs.

Having your own personal brand and your own personal community helps create value for the other party. You may have access to people they want to get in front of for one reason or another.

You must believe in yourself and that connecting with them benefits them as much as it benefits you.

Chapter 39

Creating Winning Partnerships

Let's take this to the next level.

Synergy is the idea that the sum is greater than its parts.

If we go out and network simply to increase our sales or get a job, get more people at an event, or generate more donations, we are missing out on the biggest benefit that networking has to offer.

As our own personal network grows, the potential for creating winning partnerships increases. Let's define what a winning partnership looks like.

A winning partnership is two people or two entities coming together and coming out ahead compared to working separately. Remember the poker analogy earlier in this book? We can change the game from one person winning and everyone else losing to everyone having the ability to improve their hand by exchanging with one another. We create more value by sharing resources rather than hoarding resources.

Here are the core components of creating a winning partnership.

Trust - This is a critical foundation that doesn't happen instantly. It is developed over time. Start small and work your way up to where both parties can learn to trust one another.

Clear expectations - Make sure that both parties are on the same wavelength. I remember when I was starting my first partnership. The attorney was meticulous about the terms because he said that partnerships are the only "ships" designed to sink. By setting clear expectations, you increase your chance of a successful partnership.

Equitable risk and reward - There should be a benefit to both parties by partnering together. There should also be a certain amount of risk or downside to both parties by the partnership not coming together. When both parties want to partner because of their own best interest, that's the sweet spot where you want to be. By each party looking after their own best interest, they are simultaneously helping their partners achieve their goals.

Self-sustaining - Both parties are ideally successful on their own but are even more successful due to the partnership. If one or both parties are overly dependent on the other, the chances of a breakdown of the partnership increases.

Fill the gaps - A winning partnership will help each party strengthen its existing weaknesses or needs. For example, our virtual event production company specializes exclusively in online events. By partnering with an audio-video company, we were able to expand our services to include hybrid events incorporating both in-person and online audiences!

Open communications - This is important, especially when things aren't going according to plan. Being upfront about what is and isn't working in the partnership is key to a successful long-term arrangement. While this is part of the clear expectations mentioned above, what I'm referring to here is ongoing throughout the duration of the partnership.

Congruent core values - Both parties should share similar values from the beginning without compromise.

There are many areas where give and take is a good thing. But when it comes to core values, it's essential that there be a close match from the start. This helps to resolve many potential conflicts before they even occur.

Genuine interest - A winning partnership is comprised of two parties who genuinely want to see the other succeed. There are times in the partnership when hardships will occur. It feels good to know that your partner is looking out for your best interest as much as you are looking out for theirs!

When I talk about partnerships, it doesn't necessarily mean you need to create a legal entity for every single one, but it's a good idea to have a partnership agreement in writing.

This creates clear expectations and responsibilities up front, reducing possible "misunderstandings" down the road.

You will find that these core components of creating a winning partnership will help you accomplish everything you ever wanted and more!

Chapter 40

Your Next Steps...

Congratulations on completing Networking Essentials for Success!

I believe it will transform the way you go about accomplishing your goals.

If you read this book straight through, I recommend you go back chapter by chapter and execute each step in order. Make sure you complete the activities as well!

Here's a recap of your networking journey. Gain clarity, adopt the right mindset, set up your systems and tools, meet new people, build strong relationships, build your personal brand and community, and create winning collaborations and partnerships!

My networking journey has produced many life-long friends, a loving and caring community, and countless business opportunities!

It's been a pleasure to spend the last 40 chapters with you. Let's stay in touch and continue the journey together! Join our community built around this book at **www.networkingessentialsforsuccess.com.**

If you enjoyed this book and would like to implement the content as part of a group of like-minded business and community leaders, join the next Networking Breakthrough Academy!

The Networking Breakthrough Academy is a 12-week program that helps you experience and implement each one of these 7 steps to reach your biggest goals quickly through relationships, community, and collaborative partnerships!

You'll learn a lot about yourself, your confidence will go through the roof, and you'll have the best team beside you to accomplish anything you aspire to!

Learn more at: **www.networkingbreakthroughacademy.com.**

I look forward to hearing about your accomplishments through networking. Feel free to connect with me on social media or send me a message at chris@chrisborja.com.

I'd love to know you better and share your successes with our growing community.

Happy networking!

ACKNOWLEDGMENTS

First, I would like to thank God for providing the vision, the purpose, and the resources for my life journey. This book is part of my ministry of bringing people together to appreciate our diversity, love one another, and serve others.

Thank you to:

My amazing wife and best friend, Belinda Borja, for being there every step of the way, lifting me up in the toughest of times, and inspiring me to complete this book.

My son Noah Borja, for his tech savvy and for helping us create a greater impact with all our businesses.

My daughter Zoe, for inspiring me to get out of my shell with her singing recital as a 4-year-old kid.

My mom Tessie Borja, for being an encourager and supporter and for helping me believe in myself.

My dad Ben Borja, for sharing all his wisdom and modeling what it is to be a good husband, father, and businessman.

My brother Michael Borja and sister Christine Torres for being amazing siblings as kids and as adults with growing families.

My publisher and mentor, Kary Oberbrunner, for leading the way and creating the pathway to clarity, influence, and impact.

Thank you to the Author Academy Elite team Felicity Fox, and Erica Foster for the support in the numerous processes involved in publishing a book.

My editor Cyndy Keller for the many extended Zoom calls to finally get this book out to the world.

My friend Beth Clark for the 9-day book writing retreat at Spruce Hill Inn and Cottages that allowed me to get this final version completed.

My coach Martyn Wood for his wisdom, prayers, words of encouragement, and confidence.

My good friend Jeff Elder for all the brainstorming sessions and focus sessions through all the variations of the book.

My friend Renee Vidor for the encouragement and accountability to complete this work.

My mentors Manny Lopez, Kimanzi Constable, Chris Hawker, and Sunny Martin. for providing critical pieces to the puzzle at the right times.

All those who helped and inspired me when I began my networking journey, Matt Byrne, Chaz Freutel, Frank Agin, Jim Bishop, Steve Baldzicki, Gino Petitti, and Bob Burg, through his book Endless Referrals.

Thank you to our growing CONNECTED Networking Group family for all the life-long friendships created through our events.

There are so many more people and communities that have made a difference in my life that I can't possibly name them all here.

If we are connected, know that I appreciate you and look forward to making this world a better place through our collective passions, skills, talents, and efforts.

We are connected, diversity is our strength, and we are better together!

If you enjoyed reading this book, you'll love the Networking Breakthrough Academy!

Quickly bridge the gap between you and your goals!

Implement the 7-steps to networking success as part of a supportive team!

All classes are hosted live on our interactive virtual platform so you can join from anywhere in the world!

Gain clarity. build unstoppable confidence, implement your systems, build your brand, and create winning partnerships!

Say goodbye to fear, anxiety, lost opportunities, chasing prospects, and rejection forever!

Learn more and enroll:

www.networkingbreakthroughacademy.com

SERVICES

- Corporate Consulting
- Sales Team Training
- Private Coaching

- Workshops
- Group Coaching
- Online Courses

Learn More:

CONNECTED

NETWORKING GROUP

Networking and Relationship Building at Its Finest

Meet at unique locations!

Grow your business through warm referrals!

Create genuine friendships!

Grow with a supportive community!

Fun and comfortable environment for both new AND seasoned networkers!

Learn new networking skills at every event!

**WE CREATE A FUN AND COMFORTABLE SPACE
FOR THE BUSINESS COMMUNITY TO MEET,
COLLABORATE, AND GROW!**

We are CONNECTED, diversity is our strength, and we are BETTER TOGETHER!

If you would like to start a CONNECTED chapter in your city, or if you would like to start your own personally branded networking group using our proven systems, complete the form at the link below.

https://www.connectednetworkinggroup.com/chapterinterest

BORJA VIRTUAL
CONFERENCES AND EVENTS

Is networking an important component for your next conference or event?

We become part of your team to create fun, engaging, revenue-generating, and community-building experiences!

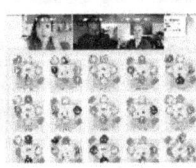

LET US HELP YOU CREATE YOUR NEXT INTERACTIVE VIRTUAL OR HYBRID EVENT!

- Conferences
- Fundraising Galas
- Networking Events
- Corporate Training
- Seminars & Workshops
- Awards & Celebrations
- Weddings & Receptions
- Expos & Trade Shows

**See our work and
SCHEDULE A DISCOVERY SESSION WITH US!**

www.borjavirtual.com

"Opening Keynote" Services

Everyone knows that networking is one of the main benefits of attending conferences, summits, and big events.

The problem is, many attendees are nervous about starting conversations with strangers, getting past the small talk, and taking full advantage of the connection opportunities with your sponsors, speakers, and each other!

As your Opening Keynote presenter, I provide inspirational story-telling, practical networking training tips, and an ice breaker activity that will get everyone out of their chairs and take the energy level of your event through the roof!

Learn more:

www.chrisborja.com/openingkeynote

Guest Appearances

Need a guest for your TV or radio show, podcast, publication, organization, or school?

Visit the link below for a media kit and to submit your request form.

www.chrisborja.com/guestrequest

BLOCKCHAIN
VERIFIED IP™

Powered by Easy IP™

CPSIA information can be obtained
at www.ICGtesting.com
Printed in the USA
BVHW050225080323
659880BV00013B/326

9 798885 831772